The
Organic
Foods
SOURCEBOOK

The
Organic
Foods
S O U R C E B O O K

Elaine Lipson

Foreword by
Kathleen A. Merrigan, Ph.D.

Contemporary Books

Chicago   New York   San Francisco   Lisbon   London   Madrid   Mexico City
Milan   New Delhi   San Juan   Seoul   Singapore   Sydney   Toronto

Library of Congress Cataloging-in-Publication Data

Lipson, Elaine.
    The organic foods sourcebook / Elaine Lipson.
      p.   cm.
   Includes bibliographical references (p.   ).
     ISBN 0-87983-978-3
    1. Natural foods—Handbooks, manuals, etc.   I. Title.
TX369 .L57 2001
641.3'02—dc21

             2001017470

Contemporary Books

A Division of The **McGraw·Hill** *Companies*

1 2 3 4 5 6 7 8 9 0 DOH/DOH 0 9 8 7 6 5 4 3 2 1

ISBN 0-87983-978-3

This book was set in Minion by Robert S. Tinnon Design
Printed and bound by R.R. Donnelley & Sons
Cover design by Laurie Young
Cover illustration by David Danz

McGraw-Hill books are available at special quantity discounts to use as premiums and sales
promotions, or for use in corporate training programs. For more information, please write
to the Director of Special Sales, Professional Publishing, McGraw-Hill, Two Penn Plaza,
New York, NY 10121-2298. Or contact your local bookstore.

For Kyle, Brennen, Sara, David, and Joely

Bless our hearts
to hear in the breaking of bread
the song of the universe.

from
One Hundred Graces: Mealtime Blessings.
Attributed to Father John Giuliani,
The Benedictine Grange,
West Redding, Connecticut

The National Organic Standards Board's
Definition of Organic Agriculture (1995)

Organic agriculture is an ecological production management system that promotes and enhances biodiversity, biological cycles, and soil biological activity. It is based on minimal use of off-farm inputs and on management practices that restore, maintain, and enhance ecological harmony. . . .
The principal guidelines for organic production are to use materials and practices that enhance the ecological balance of natural systems and that integrate the parts of the farming system into an ecological whole. . . .
The primary goal of organic agriculture is to optimize the health and productivity of interdependent communities of soil life, plants, animals, and people.

Contents

CONTENTS

Contents

Foreword

"You are what you eat!" admonished my mother as I was growing up. Maybe yours did too. Now that I'm a parent, I find myself passing on this age-old wisdom to my children. Not only do I want them to eat a nutritionally balanced diet, rich in fruits and vegetables, but I also want them to use their "food dollar" to support small farmers and organically produced foods. When they're a little older, I'll pass along another old saying that I've taken to heart—"Eating is a political act!"

Our food choices matter. They can make the difference in whether small farmers survive in an increasingly industrialized, corporate world. They can determine whether animals are humanely raised. They can significantly reduce the amount of toxic chemicals in our soil and streams.

This book explains why it is important to buy organic food. The U.S. Department of Agriculture (USDA) estimates that more than 12,000 farmers produce organic food and the vast majority of them are small, independent operators. Found in every state, producing almost every known food item, these farmers have been research pioneers—their farms are de facto natural science experiments in an era otherwise dominated by chemical-dependent agriculture. In addition to producing food, organic farmers produce knowledge about environmentally sound agricultural practices that benefits all farmers seeking to reduce synthetic pesticide and fertilizer use.

Consumers have lots of questions about organic foods. What does the organic label really mean? How does it differ from pesticide-free? Can organic foods be genetically engineered? Is it worth paying those few extra cents for the organic product? How can I be sure I'm getting what I paid for? Answers to these and other questions are provided in this book, along with a vivid critique of a pesticide regulatory system that has failed to adequately protect our children.

The USDA is poised to implement a National Organic Program in the summer of 2002 that will be a culmination of one of the most intensive public debates in USDA's history. A record-breaking 325,000 people wrote letters to the USDA commenting on how organic food should be defined and the rules that should be followed in its production and handling. Clearly people care about organic food, and estimates are that the market is growing at 20 percent annually. The USDA, after years of hostility toward organic agriculture, has come full circle and now recognizes its value to farmers, consumers, and in international trade, where demand for U.S. organic products is skyrocketing.

Whether it's at a local farmers market, within a community-supported agriculture organization, at a fancy restaurant, or at your grocery store, seek out organic food alternatives. Doing so makes the world a better place.

KATHLEEN A. MERRIGAN

Former administrator for the Agricultural Marketing Service of the U.S. Department of Agriculture, she also served as an environmental representative to the National Organic Standards Board and was awarded the Organic Trade Association Leadership Award in 2000 for her leadership and vision in furthering the goals of organic agriculture.

Acknowledgments

Thanks to Peter Hoffman, my editor at Keats/Lowell House, for his patience and support, good timing, good humor, and brilliant taste in music. I'm also very grateful to all the Keats staff who worked on this project, to Nancy Hirshberg at Stonyfield Farm, and to Thomas Hirsch, formerly of Keats, for planting the seeds for this book.

Thanks to all the organic farmers who have taught me so much, especially my brother, Mark Lipson; his wife, Marcy Abrams; and their partners at Molino Creek Farming Collective in Davenport, California, for always welcoming me and for helping me to see, over time, the importance of their endeavor and the depth of their commitment.

Thanks to the pioneers, the advocates, and the advocacy groups, formal and informal, who have dedicated themselves to changing our food system and protecting our health and environment. I'm especially grateful to Bob Scowcroft and the staff of the Organic Farming Research Foundation, Katherine DiMatteo and the staff of the Organic Trade Association, and Kathleen Downey at the Organic Materials Review Institute for generosity with resources, knowledge, and encouragement.

I'm grateful to the editors who have published my articles on organic foods and agriculture in *Delicious!, Natural Foods Merchandiser, California Certified Organic Farmers Quarterly, GreatLife,* and *Natural Business.* Portions of some of those articles have been adapted for material in this book. Special thanks to Karen Raterman at *Natural Foods Merchandiser;* Kathryn Arnold, formerly at *Delicious!* (now at *Yoga Journal*); and Lynn Prowitt-Smith, formerly at *GreatLife.*

Thanks to all the extraordinarily talented and committed people in the natural products and organic foods industries who have supported this project and provided their knowledge and encouragement. Warmest thanks and appreciation also go to some dear friends who have always shown faith in me: Julie Grusin-Mullen, Sigrid and Greg Meiris, Marilyn Murphy, Steve Conn, Howard Schiffer, Aimee and Dave Snow, Mary Scott, Lisa Turner, the Wizansky family, David Hill, Dave Kopplin, Carol McKirnan, and Ed Ross.

Last, but most important, my deepest thanks and great love go to my family for their incredible support, positive strength, understanding, and generosity: my wonderful mother, Laurie Lipson; my Lincoln family, Roger, Tracy, Kyle, Brennen, and Sara; and once again, Mark Lipson and Marcy Abrams.

Introduction

Organic choices are everywhere today. In supermarkets, farmers markets, and natural foods stores and through community-supported agriculture, organic food and fiber products have become an intrinsic part of the shopper's landscape. There are organic fruits and vegetables, of course. But there are also organic dairy products, organic meats, organic cotton clothes, organic canned foods and convenience foods, and organic wine, beer, chocolate, coffee, and tea.

This plethora of organic choices is the fruit of decades of labor, innovation, and revolution by farmers and food advocates. Consumers have responded so enthusiastically to this safer, more responsible, and more responsive food production system that what was once a fringe movement is now entering the mainstream. Yet no matter how familiar the organic label is becoming, many consumers still have only a vague understanding of what it means.

For the most part, these items cost a bit more than conventional foods. What makes them worth it? Does organic mean the same as pesticide-free? Is it better for me and for the environment, and why? Why are organic products more expensive than those grown conventionally? How can I buy organic on a budget? How do I know if it's really organic? What is "certified organic"? Is organic food safe? These are just a few of the questions this book will answer. If you have even vague concerns about the potential effects of pesticides and chemicals on your health and the environment, a clear understanding of what organic means will make it easier to shop wisely and confidently, making the best choices for you and your family.

I believe the organic choice is the best food choice available today. Organic farmers and environmental and health activists have dedicated themselves to creating an alternative to a conventional food and agriculture system that they believed was failing them and failing consumers. These pioneers have struggled to build and define a new system founded on our right to know how our food is grown and processed, what might be added to it, and how it enhances or degrades the planet we depend on. There is a profound human drama in cultivating the land and growing the food we eat every day; the fight to turn back a chemical tide and re-create a true agriculture is at its very heart.

Modern supermarkets have distanced us almost entirely from this fundamental drama, but consumers have proved with voices and dollars that they, too, want a food system that offers substantially more than chemicals and preservatives. The result is the growing organic market we have today, the fastest-growing segment of the grocery industry.[1] But the growing organic foods industry is not perfect, and consumers must still bear the responsibility of knowing where their food comes from, what its labels mean, and where it fits into a wholesome diet. Organic junk food is still better, in my opinion, than junk food made with conventionally grown ingredients and processed with chemicals.[2] For the health of your body and your budget, however, you still have to make positive, disciplined choices about healthful foods.

For healthy adults, though, the single most important reason to choose certified organic foods is this: *Organic agriculture preserves, protects, and restores our environment in significant ways*. That's true for organic chips and salsa, organic chocolate, organic coffee, and organic beer as well as for organic fruits and vegetables. Because we've lost so much of our connection to agriculture, it's easy to forget that all these things originate on farms, plantations, and ranches. Making that connection anew is essential to understanding the value of the organic label.

This book is based on the premise that the way our food is grown and processed and the choices we make about the food we buy matter. It matters to our health and well-being and to the safety and preservation of our natural environment, including soil, air, water, and other creatures. It matters to small and family farmers, now nearly completely gone from our cultural and geographic landscape, who deserve our gratitude and respect. It matters to our communities. It matters to our appreciation of life and our understanding of where food comes from.

It may matter most of all to our children. Many of the chemicals used to grow and process food today once showed great promise for efficiency in production, but we banked on that promise too soon, without understanding all the long-term effects. Few chemicals have been adequately tested, and those that have were analyzed in terms of their effect on adults. But children's developing bodies are far more vulnerable to the detrimental effects from cumulative residues. We are just beginning to analyze the risk to children.

This book is not intended to scare you or make you feel guilty. It will help you understand what organic really is, why it matters, and where to find it, in the hope that you will endorse this kind of food production. With just a few organic choices each week, you can begin to make a difference, and the quality of your food will be as good or better than it has been. You will be contributing to a healthier environment and, often, to the survival of small farms. You can do it on a budget, and you may even be inspired to start an organic kitchen garden of your own.

I also want to encourage you to learn about the food that grows in your own region and to visit an organic farm. At the very least, visit a nearby farmers market when you can and talk with the farmers there. I have the great good fortune to have a brother who became a farmer, and through my visits to the land he owns with his partners, I began to understand some of what it means to farm. It has changed my relationship with food and with the land. I hope I can now share some of that understanding with you.

CHAPTER ONE

What Organic Really Means

Organic describes a way of growing food. It's a form of agriculture, based on stewardship of the land, that arose in the last century in response to the increasing use of synthetic and often toxic chemicals to grow food. The rise in chemical agriculture in turn created a system of large-scale factory farming, while small and family farms suffered a decline. Although not all organic farms are small farms, organic agriculture is an alternative that can help small farms thrive in the wake of factory farming, benefiting our communities as well as the health of our land and people.

Yet organic farming, even when conducted on small farms, is a modern enterprise. It's often misinterpreted as an unsophisticated, old-fashioned kind of farming, where the seed is planted and pretty much left alone to do its thing. Some precursors to what we now call organic farming may have begun in this hit-and-miss fashion several decades ago, but organic agriculture has now evolved into an extremely viable alternative to conventional farming that, through scientific plant and soil cultivation, offers excellent yields to the farmer and meets the highest standards of quality and flavor.[1]

Indeed, organic food is often the preferred choice of gourmet chefs today. One old stereotype about organic food is that it's ugly, shriveled, wormy, spotted, and even bruised. This is one myth that can absolutely be put to rest. Organic food is often the freshest and most flavorful food available anywhere. And through a commitment to biodiversity, organic farmers often raise varieties of fruits, vegetables, and grains that would otherwise be lost to us. This offers an abundance of choice that big conventional growers cannot match, because this kind of diversity is anathema to the principles of sameness and hyperefficiency that guide factory farming. Organic food may not always have the illusion of a perfect appearance that conventionally grown supermarket foods have, but many consumers prefer flavor in a naturally rich package to mediocrity in a superficially perfect package.

Another very common misconception is that organic food only means "grown without chemicals." Organic does mean, in part, a system of agriculture that does not rely on synthetic pesticides, herbicides, and fertilizers. But to fully appreciate the value of organic farming and its scope as a meaningful alternative, we need to see the whole picture. True organic farming means much more than the absence of pesticides.

THE OFFICIAL DEFINITION

The National Organic Standards Board (NOSB), a government-appointed panel that advises the National Organic Program, wrote this definition of organic farming in 1995:

> Organic agriculture is an ecological production management system that promotes and enhances biodiversity, biological cycles, and soil biological activity. It is based on minimal use of off-farm inputs and on management practices that restore, maintain, and enhance ecological harmony. . . . The principal guidelines for organic production are to use materials and practices that enhance the ecological balance of natural systems and that integrate the parts of the farming system into an ecological whole. . . . The primary goal of organic agriculture is to optimize the health and productivity of interdependent communities of soil life, plants, animals, and people.[2]

To the consumer, this means that farms are managed with a different set of priorities than conventional farms use. The phrase "minimal use of off-farm inputs" refers to the fact that organic farming does not rely on synthetic pesticides, herbicides, and fertilizers.

Clearly, though, this is just one part of a larger and more profound vision of agriculture. Organic farming must by definition actively promote the health of the soil, conservation of resources, and a diversity of species on the farm. And it must respect and optimize the health and productivity of every interconnected form of life.

This is the drama and the revolution inherent in organic farming and absent in conventional, chemical-based agriculture—what we've come to call *agribusiness* for its massive scale, chemical dependency, and promotion of efficiency at the expense of sustainability. To understand the immensity of chemical use and the degree to which the conventional food system depends on these chemicals, John Wargo, in *Our Children's Toxic Legacy: How Science and Law Fail to Protect Us from Pesticides,* says, "As we approach the twenty-first century, an additional 5 to 6 billion pounds of insecticides, herbicides, fungicides, rodenticides, and other biocides are added to the world's environment each year, with roughly one-quarter of this amount released or sold in the United States."[3]

Even pesticides outlawed for use in the United States because of health risks are widely used in other countries. When food grown with these chemicals is imported back into the United States, the "circle of poison," as it has come to be known, is complete. In addition to the exposure we risk, the environmental consequences are severe in developing countries.[4]

WHY SUPPORT ORGANIC?

By examining what makes organic farming different, we also get a closer look at the benefits of organic agriculture.

Organic farming protects the health and fertility of the soil. The health of the soil is first and foremost for organic farmers. Chemically intensive practices deplete topsoil, making it essentially a vehicle to hold up the plant as artificial nutrients, pesticides, and herbicides are applied (and which can remain in the soil for many years to come).[5] Organic farming yields healthy plants by building healthy, rich soil that improves with time and good farming.

Organic farming protects the purity of the water supply. Chemicals used in farming, through runoff, have resulted in widespread contamination of groundwater and surface water, leading to detectable residues in drinking water. Wargo describes one study:

> In a 1989 analysis of "raw" (pre-treatment) and "finished" (post-treatment) drinking water from surface supplies in Illinois, Iowa, Kansas, and Ohio, the herbicides alachlor, atrazine, cyanazine, metolachlor, and 2,4-D were found in 67 percent of the raw and finished samples tested. EPA has classified all of these compounds as possible or probable human carcinogens. Atrazine in particular was found in raw water in 77 percent of the Illinois samples, 93 percent of Iowa samples, and 100 percent of Kansas samples.[6]

Organic farming does not contribute to this wholesale adulteration of our water supply, which, of course, is difficult to contain. Water eventually makes its way to the ocean, where the chemicals affect fish habitats; for this reason, even the Center for Marine Conservation advocates organic farming.[7]

Organic farming promotes biodiversity. By definition, organic farmers encourage a diversity of species rather than practicing monocropping, the widespread practice of growing one thing year after year on "factory farms," eventually depleting the soil of valuable nutrients. The resulting imbalance means that the soil is exhausted and fallow and cannot be used unless restored and that other life-forms on the farm are diminished.[8] Biodiversity helps create harmonious ecosystems with natural pest controls and contributes to thriving rather than endangered species. This respect for a multiplicity of species also means that the forms of organic agriculture that involve animal husbandry—such as dairy farming and cattle and chicken ranching—require humane treatment of herds.

Organic farming tends to be smaller in scale. Conventional farms are often owned by multinational corporations and run to hundreds of thousands of acres. By contrast, most organic farms are small or family operated; even the largest organic farms top out at about 5,000 acres right now.[9] Many organic food processors source ingredients from family farms as a guiding principle. As a result, the growing marketplace for organic has given many small farms a lifeline that they would not otherwise have.

Pesticides in food and the environment are a real threat to children's health. Pesticides in use in the United States have, by and large, been evaluated by the Environmental Protection Agency (EPA) for their short-term, individual effects on healthy adult males. New evidence suggests that we should be demanding evaluation of multiple pesticides as they accumulate over time, more closely mimicking the way these chemicals are actually used and introduced into the human body. Furthermore, these chemicals may be especially toxic for young children, whose nervous systems are still developing. Children eat proportionally more fruits and vegetables than adults and so ingest more pesticide residue in relation to their overall diet. Although the Food Quality Protection Act (FQPA) of 1996 mandates reassessment of risk for commonly used pesticides, a slow pace for review and loopholes in the law mean that these pesticides are still in use under the same distorted umbrella of "safety." [10, 11]

Pesticides in food and the environment add to a toxic burden that may contribute to increases in some forms of cancer, an increased incidence of allergies and asthma, and other health problems. Again, past methods of risk assessment for pesticides are continually being revealed as inadequate. Some chemicals have the potential to cause serious consequences over time, or over generations of use. The cumulative and exponential effects of multiple pesticides, along with exposure to other toxins in the environment, create a load of toxins that has inevitable effects on the human body. Farmworkers, not surprisingly, suffer from excessive chemical exposure; under pressure to produce, farmers are not always able to observe the necessary precautions.

Organic food is often the freshest, most flavorful food in the marketplace. Those who grew up with foods fresh from the farm say they hardly recognize the foods they see in modern supermarkets, devoid of real taste and freshness. Organic foods at their best bring back all that food is supposed to be: flavor sensations made manifest by rich soil, clean water, and sun instead of chemical concoctions.

SUMMARY

- Organic farming is a modern system of food production that does not use toxic and persistent chemicals and that actively promotes ecological integrity.
- Organic farming protects the health and fertility of the soil.
- Organic farming helps protect the cleanliness of groundwater and the water supply by eliminating chemical runoff.
- Organic farming promotes and conserves biological diversity.
- Organic farming can be a lifeline for small and family farms and an alternative to large-scale agribusiness, with its environmental and social consequences.
- Organic foods are grown without the use of pesticides and other chemicals, many of which are now being reevaluated for health risks to children and which add to the overall burden of environmental toxins.
- Organic foods are often the freshest, most flavorful foods in the marketplace.

CHAPTER TWO

"Pesticides Are Harmless"
and Ten More Misconceptions
About Organic Foods and
Organic Farming

Myth #1
Organic is the same as pesticide-free.

Truth
"Pesticide-free" is a misnomer, and even if it were accurate, organic agriculture is much more than the absence of pesticides.

Organic means, in part, an agricultural and food production process that does not rely on synthetic pesticides, herbicides, and fertilizers. A few synthetic materials are permitted in organic farming, usually for very specific uses, as a last resort to protect a crop when no natural equivalent is available to the farmer.[1] But organic is more than the absence of pesticides.

The label "pesticide-free" is inaccurate and can be misleading. Sadly, virtually nothing on this earth is truly free of pesticide residues after decades of pouring these chemicals into our soil, air, and water, where they are not contained and do not disappear. Pesticides are in all of our bodies, even if we eat organic food, and they have been found in virtually every corner of the earth.[2, 3] Decades after the pesticide DDT was outlawed for use, its toxic residues can still be found. Organic food is intended to be as free from pesticides as possible, but it's far too late in the course of agribusiness's wholesale dedication to these synthetic materials for any guarantees.

Finally, certified organic foods must have a written trail of information telling the consumer exactly how the food was grown and processed and what independent party verified its claims. A "pesticide-free" label, since no requirements govern it, may not have this same documentation. Stores and growers using the "pesticide-free" label may not be trying to be deceptive, but consumers should not interpret the label as meaning the same thing as the organic label. (See chapter 7 for more information on eco-labels and how to evaluate them.)

With all that said, some very responsible and conscientious farmers use the phrase "pesticide-free." I buy sweet corn from Munson's Farm near my home in Boulder, Colorado, and they use this phrase. I wish they'd use different language, and I wish they'd go 100 percent certified organic. But I know this farm, their practices, and their loyalty to farming in this region, and I'm confident, from talking to them directly, that I understand what they mean by this claim. If you buy foods labeled pesticide-free, be sure you have this same level of confidence.

Myth #2
Everything in a natural foods store is organic.

Truth
Most natural foods stores sell both organically grown and conventionally grown foods, although most restrict the use of chemical preservatives and additives.

If you shop at a natural foods or health foods store, you may think that everything you're buying is organic. It's a common misconception that these stores sell exclusively organic items. But for the most part, while they have standards that limit what they'll sell in the store, they are offering a mix of foods that are organic and those that are not. These are what we've come to know as "natural" foods. The ingredient list is all recognizable, with no multisyllabic chemical preservatives, but ingredients may be conventionally farmed and even genetically engineered. And in the produce section, most of these stores offer both conventionally and organically grown foods, usually marked and hopefully segregated so that chemically grown foods are not contaminating organic selections. Finally, don't assume that prepared foods from the deli section of your natural foods store are made from organic ingredients.

Choices that are not organic but that fall into the "natural" category do offer freedom from preservatives and artificial ingredients. But if you have an understanding of what organic really means and you want to consciously support environmentally healthy choices and an alternative to chemical farming, look for the certified organic label whenever you can. (To learn more about where to buy organic foods, see chapter 10.)

Myth #3
Organic foods mean only fresh fruits and vegetables.

Truth
There's an organic choice in almost every food and beverage category and in many products made with cotton.

Organic standards have been developed for nearly every kind of food and drink. This includes coffee, chocolate, sugar, pasta, grains, wine grapes, oils, tea, and nuts. We also now have organic standards for dairy products, meat, and poultry. And don't forget fiber. Beautiful organically grown cotton is now available for clothing and home textiles.[4]

You can also make the organic choice when buying processed foods, from baby foods to cereals to canned, frozen, and convenience foods. In these cases, the processing standards are certified as well as the growing methods. (For more on the many organic items available, see chapter 9.)

Myth #4
There's no way of knowing if something is really organic.

Truth
Certification has been, and remains, the consumer's best independent verification and guarantee.

It's true that in many states, for many years, anyone could use the organic label without verification or oversight of farming and production practices. But even then, state and private certification agencies gave consumers the option of buying certified organic. In late 2000, the United States Department of Agriculture issued a final national standard for any food with the organic label, for implementation in 2002. (For more on organic certification and what the organic standards mean for consumers, see chapter 6.)

Myth #5

Organic food is unsafe because they use manure on crops.

Truth

Manure use is strictly regulated in organic production—more so than in conventional farming.

Food safety is one of the biggest consumer concerns today, and at least one antiorganic think tank is using this frightening argument to discredit organic food. The use of appropriately processed manure—the only kind allowed in certified organic practices—is a time-honored farming practice and a safe one, as heat destroys any harmful pathogens in the raw manure. The fact is that manure is used to fertilize all kinds of farms, not just organic farms. And the United States Department of Agriculture's (USDA) national organic standard makes organic farming the *only* form of agriculture in this country with strict regulations for how manure is treated and used.[5]

Food safety is a concern with every form of food production today. Most of the recent cases of illness from *E. coli H:157* have not been from organic foods, but rather from contaminated meats, contaminated water supplies, and unpasteurized juice. That said, the organic label is not a food safety claim; this means that every consumer should follow sensible food safety precautions for all foods. If your family includes children under six years of age, seniors, or anyone with a compromised immune system, follow food safety rules with special vigilance. This means, for example, cooking meat thoroughly, washing all produce, not allowing raw meats to contact other foods or cutting surfaces, and using only pasteurized juice.[6] (For more information on methods of organic farming, see chapter 4.)

Myth #6

Organic food costs twice as much as conventionally grown food.

Truth

Organic foods usually do cost more than conventional foods, but rarely 100 percent more, and savvy consumers can buy organic without breaking the bank.

Organic food does cost more than conventionally grown food most of the time. But the premium is usually closer to 15 or 20 percent, not 100 percent. If organic food is marked up that much, it's likely to be out of season and imported. Consider making food choices that are seasonal and local to bring costs down and bring you closer to natural seasonal cycles and your own climate and community.

Understanding why organic costs more and the benefits of organic food and agriculture can help you make good choices and set spending priorities. There are also ways to buy organic even on a budget. (See chapter 13 for more on this topic.)

Myth #7

Organic foods are ugly, shriveled, brown, and wormy.

Truth

Organic foods are often some of the freshest, most flavorful foods available.

If you've been to a farmers market or a natural foods store lately, you know that organic foods are often the freshest, most flavorful and appealing foods available today. Organic tomatoes, for example, are really red when ripe, not a washed-out orange-red color. While cookie-cutter perfection is not the goal of organic farmers, most organic foods sold through reputable farmers or retailers knowledgeable about organic foods are exactly what food should be—bursting with flavor and nutrients from naturally rich soil.

Conventional agribusiness breeds crops for certain traits, such as uniformity in appearance, slow ripening, and long shelf life, all of which allows foods to be warehoused longer, trucked more miles, and even stacked more closely. Quality, flavor, and variety are lower priorities. Sadly, we've become so accustomed to food that profits the supermarket rather than pleases the palate that we hardly trust food that doesn't meet this code of uniformity. As you explore the world of organic foods, your thinking is likely to change; you may even begin to appreciate some of the more unusual heirloom vegetables that some organic farmers grow today.

Myth #8

Organic food is just for rich people.

Truth

We need to work for a food system that allows safe food for everyone and respects everyone's right to know how food is grown and produced.

Every community shares the values that created and sustained the organic farming and foods movement. Everyone has the right to safe food and to complete disclosure of how it was grown and processed. Everyone has the right to know the full array of potential effects of chemicals used in food production and agricultural methods. And everyone has the right to know if the land, water, and air that is part of their community will be affected by chemical degradation and to participate, if they choose, in protecting those resources.

There is no doubt that organic food at the retail level has been marketed primarily to affluent communities. I hope very much to see that change in the near future. Until then, advocates working for community food safety, farmers bringing food directly to market, and farsighted grocers may help make natural and organic foods more available to medium- and low-income and inner-city communities. In too many cases, these neighborhoods must bear a toxic burden that affluent communities have the clout to drive elsewhere, but it shouldn't be that way in the grocery store too. (For more on buying organic on a budget, see chapter 13.)

Myth #9

Organic farmers are making tons of money.

Truth

Most organic farmers, like small and family farmers who use conventional methods, don't have the luxury of large profits.

Because organic food generally costs more at the retail level, many buyers assume that organic farmers are making a killing. In fact, most organic farmers gross less than $30,000 each year from organic farming.[7] The more you as a consumer support organic agriculture, the more you may help provide a market for many small and family farmers who are less and less able to compete against large factory farms in the conventional market. (For more on family farming, small farms, and organic farmers, see chapter 8.)

Myth #10
I don't have to buy organic. Pesticides in the food supply are safe because the government says so.

Truth
There are legitimate concerns about pesticides in use today and those previously banned but still persistent; about the way pesticide tolerances have been evaluated; and, in particular, about risks to infants and children from pesticides considered "safe" in our food supply.

Pesticides may not be visible, but many are far from harmless to either the environment or human health, especially children's health. In fact, the Food Quality Protection Act (FQPA) of 1996 mandated the reevaluation, over time, of risk for all agricultural chemicals. Although the government has told us that these chemicals are safe, the EPA has now acknowledged that the way that tolerance has been evaluated has been inadequate.

Furthermore, some chemicals stay in the soil for decades, even after they've been banned from use. For example, a study published in the *Journal of Agricultural and Food Chemistry* analyzing produce grown in soil that had been treated with chlordane, an organochlorine pesticide, thirty-eight years earlier found residues in all twelve vegetables harvested.[8] Chlordane, like DDT, has been banned for use in this country, but continues to contaminate our food through its persistence in soil and water.

Conventionally grown food will never bear a label informing you which pesticides have been used to produce it. But it doesn't take much digging to unearth very real concerns about pesticide residues in this food.

And that doesn't even begin to take into account the damage that these chemicals do to the environment, including wildlife. (For more on why pesticide use should concern you, see chapters 5 and 14.)

Myth #11
Organic farming can't feed the world.

Truth
Investments in organic farming research may prove otherwise.

Companies that profit from the production and sale of agricultural chemicals and proprietary genetically modified seeds and crops like to broadcast the misconception that organic farming can't sustain large populations. In fact, very little research has been done to measure the real capacity of organic agriculture.[9] Some studies show that organic farms have a better yield in drought years than conventional farms and that organic yields in general can be compatible with conventional farms.[10] Furthermore, organically farmed soil has a future rather than being depleted by chemically driven imbalances, so it can continue to yield nutritious food rather than becoming fallow. Finally, organic farming remains a lifeline for small and family farmers in developing countries as well as in the United States, so that farmers can feed families and communities and remain independent of multinational chemical manufacturers—an option that honors diverse ways of life and culture as well as the biological diversity that organic agriculture supports. (For more on organic farming methods, see chapter 4. For a discussion of genetic modification in agriculture, see chapter 12.)

We all think we know what we need to about food. After all, it's an integral part of our survival and enjoyment of life. But in fact, when it comes to our food, what you see—and what you think you're getting—is not always what you get. It may be easier to stay uninformed, but a greater understanding of what is and is not in our food can be truly rewarding in the long run. If you're buying organic or considering switching to more organic foods in your kitchen, knowing what organic really means and what the misconceptions are benefits you, your family, and ultimately your community and our collective home on earth.

SUMMARY

Myths and misconceptions about organic foods abound. Savvy consumers know that:

- A pesticide-free label does not mean the same thing as the organic label.
- Not everything in a natural foods store is organic.
- There are organic choices in almost every food category, as well as organic fiber products (primarily cotton).
- Organic certification is a consumer's guarantee of organic practices, and national standards for organic certification were finalized in 2000 for 2002 implementation.
- Compost use in organic agriculture is regulated for safety under USDA regulations, although food safety practices should always be followed for all kinds of foods.
- Organic foods often do cost more, but offer higher quality and other benefits. It's possible to buy organic on a budget, especially as supply and availability increase.
- Consumers can have legitimate concerns about pesticide exposure and health, especially for children.
- The potential of organic farming is still relatively unexplored. With research, we can learn more about the viability of organic farming as a global food production solution.

CHAPTER THREE

Eleven Reasons to Support Organic Foods and Farming

This quick reference list is adapted from "Top Ten Reasons to Buy Organic" by Sylvia R. Tawse, originally written in 1992 for Alfalfa's Markets, a Colorado natural foods chain. Today, it still stands as a clear, succinct overview of the many benefits of organic food and farming that's hard to improve on. I've updated information where appropriate and added reason 11. Thanks to the Organic Trade Association and Sylvia R. Tawse for permission to adapt her list.[1]

1. PROTECT FUTURE GENERATIONS

Children receive four times more exposure than adults to at least eight widely used cancer-causing pesticides found in foods. The food choice you make now will impact your child's health in the future.

2. PREVENT SOIL EROSION

The Soil Conservation Service estimates that more than 3 billion tons of topsoil are eroded from U.S. croplands each year. That means soil is eroding seven times faster than it is built up naturally. Soil is the foundation of the food chain in organic farming, but in conventional farming the soil is used more as a medium for holding plants in a vertical position so they can

---

be chemically fertilized. As a result, American farms are suffering from the worst soil erosion in history.

3. PROTECT WATER QUALITY

Water makes up two-thirds of our body mass and covers three-fourths of the planet. Despite water's importance, the EPA estimates that pesticides contaminate groundwater in at least thirty-eight states, polluting the primary source of drinking water for more than half the country's population.

4. SAVE ENERGY

American farms have changed drastically in the last three generations, from the family-based small business to the large-scale factory farm highly dependent on fossil fuels. Modern farming uses more petroleum than any other single industry, consuming 12 percent of the country's total energy supply. More energy is now used to produce synthetic fertilizers than to till, cultivate, and harvest all the crops in the United States. Organic farming is based on practices such as using crop covers rather than synthetic inputs. Organic produce also tends to travel a shorter distance from the farm to your plate.

5. KEEP CHEMICALS OFF YOUR PLATE

Many pesticides approved for use by the EPA were registered before extensive research linking these chemicals to cancer and other diseases had been established. Now the EPA considers that 60 percent of all herbicides, 90 percent of all fungicides, and 30 percent of all insecticides are carcinogenic. There are associations between pesticide use and cancer among farmers and in farm communities. The bottom line is that pesticides are poisons designed to kill living organisms that can also be harmful to humans. In addition to contributing to the incidence of cancer, pesticides are implicated in birth defects, nerve damage, and genetic mutation.

6. PROTECT FARMWORKERS' HEALTH

A National Cancer Institute study found that farmers exposed to herbicides had a greater risk than nonfarmers of contracting cancer—by a factor of six. In California, reported pesticide poisonings among farmworkers have risen an average of 14 percent a year since 1973 and doubled between 1975 and 1985. Field workers suffer the highest rates of occupational illness in the state. Farmworker health is also a serious problem in developing nations, where pesticide use can be poorly regulated. An estimated 1 million people are poisoned annually by pesticides. Several of the pesticides banned for use in the United States are still manufactured here for export to other countries (and food grown with those chemicals is often imported back into the United States in what has become known as the "circle of poison").

7. HELP SMALL FARMERS

Although more and more large-scale farms are making the conversion to organic practices, most organic farms are small, independently owned and operated family farms of less than 100 acres. It's estimated that the United States has lost more than 650,000 family farms in the past decade. As food production becomes increasingly concentrated, controlled by fewer and larger companies, the market offered through organic farming could become one of the few hopes left for family farms.

8. SUPPORT A TRUE ECONOMY

Although organic foods might seem more expensive than conventional foods, conventional food prices do not reflect hidden costs borne by taxpayers, including billions of dollars in federal subsidies that help control crop prices and the food supply. Other hidden costs include pesticide regulation and testing, hazardous waste disposal and cleanup, and environmental damage and the costs of mitigating or reversing it.

9. PROMOTE BIODIVERSITY

Monocropping is the practice of planting large plots of land with the same crop year after year. While this approach tripled farm production between 1950 and 1970, the lack of natural diversity of plant life has left the soil lacking in natural minerals and nutrients. To replace the nutrients, chemical fertilizers are used, often in increasing amounts.

10. FRESHNESS AND FLAVOR

There's a good reason why many chefs use organic foods in their recipes. They often taste better. Organic farming starts with the nutrients of the soil, which eventually leads to the nourishment of the plant and ultimately our palates.

11. KNOW HOW YOUR FOOD IS GROWN AND AVOID GENETICALLY MODIFIED INGREDIENTS

Up to two-thirds of foods in today's grocery stores may contain genetically modified ingredients, with foreign genes spliced into plants to create characteristics that serve the needs of agribusiness rather than consumers. Though the process of genetic engineering in agriculture may pose serious threats to environmental health and even to human health, little research has been done with regard to long-term risks, and no labeling is required. Organic farming provides an audit trail of certification from seed to shelf; growers document how the farm is run, exactly what inputs are used, and other relevant information. At the present time, the organic label is a consumer's only assurance that foods are grown without the use of genetic engineering and that federal regulations back up that claim.

SUMMARY

There are many positive reasons to support organic foods and farming. They include:

- Environmental reasons—Organic farming helps prevent topsoil erosion, ensure soil fertility, protect groundwater, conserve biological diversity, and conserve energy.
- Social reasons—Small and family farms are at risk, and organic agriculture offers one option that can help them survive.
- Health reasons—Chemicals in the ground, air, water, and food supply are associated with health consequences from asthma to cancer. Organic farming helps to limit this toxic burden.
- Pure pleasure—Organic foods offer freshness, flavor, and quality (and, in the best-case scenario, a real sense of connection to where our food comes from).

CHAPTER FOUR

Principles of Organic Agriculture

Organic farming is more than the absence of pesticides. Viewing organic agriculture as simply farming without chemicals ignores an entire set of principles that make organic farming beneficial to the environment instead of just not damaging it. If organic farming echoed conventional farming and just skipped the chemicals, it probably would be a dismal failure. But far from just omitting harmful substances, organic farmers actively cultivate healthy ecosystems. This is exactly why the label "pesticide-free" is not the equivalent of "organic" and leaves consumers with a lot of questions; it tells only part of the story.

Principles of organic agriculture include, first and foremost, an attention to soil health and fertility. A commitment to biodiversity—a diverse variety of plants and animals on the farm, rather than a single crop without natural balances—is also a key element of organic agriculture. Interdependency—the concept that all life on the farm is connected and that affecting one life-form will also affect others—leads to the concept of wholeness, that all life on the farm is integrated into an ecological whole. Within the framework of this ecological whole, specific techniques of efficient energy and resource use, healthy animal husbandry, and ecological pest and weed control with minimal off-farm inputs may vary from farm to farm and crop to crop, depending on appropriate activities for the climate and region.

SECRETS OF THE SOIL

Every gardener knows that good soil is the key to success. In organic agriculture, the health and fertility of the soil become paramount. Conventional growers often use soil as simply a vehicle to physically hold up the plant, with chemical fertilizers providing nutrition. Soil often becomes unbalanced and even depleted from monoculture practices, in which only one type of crop is grown year after year. Vital topsoil becomes eroded, sometimes at alarming rates.

Organic farmers pay close attention to soil as the primary source of the plant's nutrition, along with water and sun. Soil is seen as a resource that, with proper cultivation, can become richer year after year instead of weaker. "Feed the soil, not the plant" is the mantra of organic growers, who seek to restore, maintain, and improve soil to reach a state of balance, fertility, and fecundity.

Healthy soil is not just "dirt" but is teeming with life. Farmers often talk about earthworms and how they multiply in soil cultivated with organic methods, but worms may just be the biggest members of the soil food web. Just one teaspoon of rich organic soil contains a multiplicity of hundreds of millions of microorganisms and soil bacteria to help nutrients cycle through it.

Healthy soil does indeed lead to healthy plants, with more disease and pest resistance and optimal nutritional value. Healthy soil may also be better able to withstand drought conditions or other adverse weather.[1]

Soil that has been used for conventional farming may have persistent chemical residues and may take time to restore to suitability for organic agriculture. For this reason, such land must spend at least three years in transition, without additional chemical inputs, before earning organic certification.

BIODIVERSITY—THE WEB OF LIFE

The earth's diversity of plants and animals (including insects and microorganisms) is not just a curiosity, but a biological necessity for a healthy planet. Biodiversity is more than just a buzzword; its decline is a critical environmental problem, and agriculture plays a major role. Conventional modern farming techniques contribute to the decline of species and genetic variety, whereas organic farming, by its very definition, promotes biodiversity.

Biodiversity, or biological diversity, is evaluated in three ways. The number of species of plants, animals, and microorganisms is perhaps the most obvious measure of diversity. Yet healthy genetic variation within each species is also critical to adaptation and survival. Biodiversity, then, is not just the number of species but also the multiplicity of differences within each one. Finally, scientists observe the diversity of ecosystems where different forms of life can thrive. "In sum," writes Gary Kline, professor of political science at Georgia Southwestern State University, "biodiversity refers to the aggregate of ecosystems, species, and genes, which together comprise life on earth."[2]

In the last century, the number of species has begun to decline precipitously. Whereas natural extinction might occur at the rate of about a dozen species per year, scientists estimate that we are currently seeing the disappearance of species at *one thousand to ten thousand times the natural rate.*[3] And while public attention focuses on appealing or exotic endangered species like snow leopards or spotted owls, the balance of life also depends on the vast diversity of plants, insects, and microorganisms.

Even using the most conservative estimate, this rate of species extinction is astonishing. Modern agriculture shares the blame with many other factors, including other forms of polluting technology, the population explosion, and the conversion of wilderness to other uses.

Does it matter? "Though we are just beginning to comprehend it, the value of biodiversity is rooted firmly in the laws of science and economics and we disregard this only at our extreme peril," Kline says.[4] In many cases, we don't even know how the species we are destroying may contribute to planetary balance—to healthy air, soil, and water, to the recycling of natural waste, and to the generation of other life. Historical experience suggests, however, that we should err on the side of caution in allowing species of unknown purpose to run dry. Biodiversity in practice strengthens ecosystems and lessens the likelihood of agricultural or other catastrophes.

A lack of diversity makes populations of any kind more vulnerable. Conventional farming techniques limit crops through selection and breeding, fostering plants that have less immunity to disease and pests and making it harder to cultivate those plants without additional chemical inputs.

Yet conventional modern agricultural techniques continue to emphasize these very strategies. By encouraging an ever-dwindling genetic base and a dependence on chemicals that indiscriminately kill other species (and then generate resistant harmful pests) or make land inhospitable for their use, modern agriculture upsets the balance of nature in the most destructive ways. "Modern agriculture has had a very detrimental effect on biodiversity," writes David E. Ervin of the Henry Wallace Institute for Alternative Agriculture. "The conversion of many grasslands and wetlands to crops, increases in size of fields and elimination of woodlands and edges, reduced crop diversity, less crop rotation, and the increased use of fertilizer and pesticides have greatly reduced animal and plant populations, even in species that are otherwise well adapted to agriculture."[5]

Agricultural impact on biodiversity extends beyond the farm itself. "On-site biodiversity can be reduced because of increased specialization and reliance on a few improved crop species," say Stefano Pagiola and coauthors, scientists at the World Bank, "while off-site damage can increase through increased use of chemical fertilizers and pesticides."[6] The "increased specialization" has reached dismaying proportions; variety in our food supply has dropped dramatically. Keith Schneider, executive director of the Michigan Land Use Institute, says that "since the early 1970s, plant breeders have worried that the abundance of the world's food supply is balanced on a narrowing supply of wild and domestic plant genes. . . . Homogenization in the market is one result. Hunger can be another."[7]

As we begin to understand the long-term consequences to biodiversity by conventional farming practices, the alternative methods of organic farming become even more valuable. The accepted definition of organic (see pages 2 and 3) makes the promotion of biodiversity an essential and primary principle of organic agriculture. In other words, if farming methods don't support biodiversity, they aren't organic.

INTERDEPENDENCY

Buddhists say that a butterfly can flutter its wings in China and cause a tidal wave halfway across the world. It's a colorful way to illustrate how every action matters and how all living things are interdependent. The same principle is embraced by organic farmers. Practices that promote health and diversity will benefit all life on the farm, while destructive practices with short-term benefits and long-term costs will have negative consequences across the board.

The lesson is hard won. When the American eagle nearly became extinct, part of the problem was that the pesticide DDT—the miraculous Nobel Prize–winning gift—was thinning the eagles' eggs so much that the species became threatened. Factory farming of coffee and cocoa beans in the tropics affects songbird populations in the Northern Hemisphere. Genetically engineered corn and soy may harm monarch butterfly populations. Pesticides harm honeybees and other pollinators. Endocrine-disrupting chemicals applied to plants move up the food chain to have a powerful impact all the way up the ladder and for future generations. These are graphic examples of how the fruitfulness and health of the entire globe may depend on the forms of agriculture we choose today.

The principles of interdependence must be applied on both this large, global scale and on smaller scales. The values of organic agriculture include balance, health, and diversity for all the species on the farm, from farmworkers to farm animals. Food transportation, storage, and processing all must be conducted with ecological values intact.

ECOLOGICAL WHOLENESS

Ecological wholeness suggests that all the diverse and interdependent parts of the system are healthy, functioning, and add up to a productive whole. This is logical from nature's point of view—it's all designed that way. Cycles of decay and creation, seasons, and other changes are synchronistic and balanced. The ongoing goal of all these principles is *sustainability,* whereby the sum total of agricultural activities replaces the resources it uses and does not degrade the earth.

Sustainable agriculture requires foresight, knowledge, innovation, research, and constant experimentation to find ways to work with nature to maximize long-term positive results without ecological harm or depletion of resources. The classic view of sustainability is to leave our children with the same gifts and opportunities of nature that we have. I would add that it also means leaving them with a historical long view, with a full and open record of mistakes, failures, detours, and dead ends as well as successes.

FROM PRINCIPLES TO PRACTICE

The specific methods that organic farmers use to manifest organic principles include, of course, rejecting reliance on synthetic chemical pesticides and fertilizers. Other techniques include cultivating a diversity of plants. By alternating and rotating crops, organic farmers keep the soil balanced while encouraging diversity. Organic farmers also effectively use cover crops to add nutrients to the soil and limit weeds without chemical inputs. By using and respecting natural boundaries such as fence rows, wetlands, woodlands, and edges, farmers encourage thriving, diverse ecosystems in and around the farm.

Nature gives us a host of additional tools to achieve the end goal of healthy, thriving food plants with minimal off-farm, or chemical, inputs. For example, organic farmers often use beneficial insects as one form of pest control. Perhaps the most famous of beneficial insects is the ladybug, which feeds on aphids, but there are many others that, when appropriate for crop and region, feed on undesirable insects without harming plants.

These insects can be released on the farm or naturally attracted to plants. Companion planting is a technique of farm or garden design whereby plants are located to bring the right beneficial insects to a particular area or, in some cases, to repel unwanted insects.

For those who would like to learn more about organic farming and even try their hand at it, there are good books, study programs, and internships available. Even some of the larger agricultural schools, with big money invested in conventional farming research, have sustainable agriculture programs and communities. Other schools may not offer conventional agriculture degrees but have innovative programs in organic farming and gardening available to nondegree students, such as the six-month program at the Center for AgroEcology at the University of California in Santa Cruz. (See Resources for information on school programs and apprenticeship/travel networks.)

Home gardens and community gardens are ideal for organic gardening, where many of the techniques of organic growing can be practiced on a small scale. Some community-supported agriculture programs also include farmwork and can offer rich learning experiences.

THE MANURE QUESTION

Organic farmers maintain soil and plant health and fertility, as well as conserving resources and improving yields, by recycling wastes into compost and manure for appropriate use as farm inputs. Using manure-based fertilizers is a time-honored technique practiced by all kinds of farmers and growers and is safe when proper safeguards are used. In fact, the strict documentation and standards required for certification as organic, under the USDA's federal law in particular, means that manure use is *more* regulated in organic farming than elsewhere.[8]

With respect to bacteria and pathogens, food safety is a concern for all food growers, processors, and consumers, no matter how the food is grown. Whether organic, transitional, or conventional, farms must use hygienic practices to maintain adequate levels of food safety. Most food-related illness comes from undercooked meat and other products. There has been one tragic incidence of fatal *E. coli* poisoning from unpasteurized juice given to a baby; media perception was that the product was organic, and concerns about the safety of organic foods were broadcast. The product was not organic. But with any food choice, it's important to understand food safety fundamentals. For example, never feed unpasteurized juice or other high-risk foods to a baby or anyone else with an undeveloped or weak immune system.

Heirloom Vegetables and Seed-Saving Exchanges

Heirloom vegetables give us a beautiful glimpse of biodiversity in action, offering a fantastic variety of beautiful, colorful fresh foods that come from the past and look like the future. From black and zebra-striped tomatoes to melons with a mystical moon and star pattern on the rind, these aren't the creations of gene modification or other space-age technology, but of treasured seeds handed down like priceless antiques.

In fact, while scientists of the twenty-first century are busily engineering vegetables for sameness and predictability—even breeding tomatoes for squareness so they'll pack and ship more easily—a dazzling world of variety and flavor waits at the other end of the vegetable spectrum in heirloom vegetables. The Brandywine tomato is the best-known heirloom variety, but there are thousands more. Grown from open-pollinated seeds passed carefully from generation to generation, heirloom vegetables are capturing the interest of consumers, growers, chefs, and retailers alike with a diversity and richness that reminds us of what vegetables once were and can be.

Often unique in appearance and intensely flavorful, true heirloom vegetables are those whose seeds have been handed down within a family or a variety that dates back at least fifty years, according to the Eastern Native Seed Conservancy (ENSC) based in Great Barrington, Massachusetts. Many heirloom seeds were carried by refugees and immigrants into the United States and delivered hand to hand through generations. "That distinguishes heirloom crops from traditional crops, which are those grown by native peoples, predominantly Native Americans," says Alan Kapuler, Ph.D., of Seeds of Change, a Santa Fe, New Mexico–based organic seeds and foods company. "Any tribal group who passed seeds on—we call those seeds traditional."[9]

Heirloom vegetables are also grown from open-pollinated seeds, or seeds that can reproduce themselves true to type. According to Seeds of Change, "Open-pollinated plants are produced from parents that are genetically identical or similar and are produced from plants which are allowed to pollinate, without human intervention, through insects, wind and water. . . . Open-pollinated plants, managed carefully, or crossed on purpose, will produce offspring with reliable characteristics, allowing seeds to be saved and grown out year after year."[10]

By contrast, conventional vegetable seeds, known as F1 hybrids, do not reproduce true to type and can even be sterile. Open-pollinated seeds and the heirloom vegetables grown from them, then, are a link to a farming and gardening tradition that precedes chemical farming and agribusiness. Though the efficiencies of large-scale modern conventional farming, with its ever-shrinking number of food varieties, are missing from the world of heirloom vegetables, they link us to cultural and spiritual traditions that can enrich not just our plates but our communities.

Yet heirloom vegetables are more than nostalgia, however passionately growers may feel about their heritage. Preserving and promoting genetic diversity remains a critical environmental concern. "As we've diminished biodiversity, we've attacked this web of interactions of organisms which provides a stable foundation for all life in the world," Kapuler says. "Diversity is the strength, and I believe the staff of life. In the last twenty years, many of the crops which are commonly available have been selected only for stability on the shelf and for appearance. In terms of diversity, it's worth it to broaden why we select and how we choose our food plants."[11]

While concepts of heritage and genetic diversity are vitally important, they can also be a bit abstract for busy people. But heirloom vegetables offer immediate gratification—succulent, intense flavor and dazzling, unusual arrays of color and appearance. Where to find them? They can occasionally be found in natural foods stores, but more often can be purchased at farmers markets or through community-supported agriculture programs (but be sure the farm you choose offers heirlooms). And you can grow your own, obtaining seeds through a seed savers exchange that lets you network with other gardeners or buying seeds from a company like Seeds of Change (see Resources).

Heirloom vegetables are often, but not necessarily, organic, though of course the seeds are likely to be untreated and certainly allow for organic methods of cultivation from seed to table. The principle of diverse elements woven through interdependence into an ecological whole, however, is well served by heirloom vegetables. They're fun, beautiful, delicious, and interesting—and they're a feast for all the senses as well as for our collective environmental conscience.

Food safety does seem more of a concern today, with new "superbugs" constantly threatening the food supply. Produce of any kind should be washed, and meat should be cooked to appropriate temperatures. Basic food safety measures should be followed, and if anyone in your household is at risk, those measures should be followed religiously. But manure use in organic farming follows strict guidelines for safety. If you follow reasonable food hygiene practices, you are no more at risk from organic foods than from other foods. And if you don't follow those practices, all foods put you at risk. The Food and Drug Administration (FDA) and Center for Science in the Public Interest (www.cspinet.org) are two good sources for basic food safety information.

SUMMARY

- Key principles of organic agriculture include soil health and fertility, biodiversity, interdependence of organisms, not relying on the use of off-farm inputs, and integrating the parts of the agricultural system into an ecological whole.
- A variety of evolving practices, such as biological pest control, cover crops, crop rotation, and recycling of wastes, contribute to organic farm management.
- Organic farming, like other farming methods, may use correctly processed manure as fertilizer, with specific guidelines outlined in certification programs and the USDA national organic standard.
- In support of biodiversity, growing, buying, and eating heirloom vegetables can be a fun, interesting way to explore the diversity of plant food species.

CHAPTER FIVE

From the Miracle of Pesticides to a New Agriculture

Are pesticides safe? They are, after all, regulated by the Environmental Protection Agency and approved for agricultural use. There's rarely an immediate cause-and-effect relationship between eating conventionally grown food and showing signs of pesticide-related illness. But many pesticides are among the most toxic chemicals in use today. Foods often arrive at grocery stores with pesticide residues that exceed the limits considered safe, especially for children, although the "average" amount of residues may well be within set limits of tolerance.

And even those limits of tolerance may be misleading. The real effects of pesticides must be measured in terms of environmental, cultural, and health costs, but also in terms of whole systems. Pesticides and other agricultural chemicals, we have learned, may be exponentially more toxic in combination than individually, yet that is exactly how they are usually used and ingested. Historically, however, they've been tested only for individual effect. And pesticides have a more powerful effect on the developing bodies of infants and children, necessitating revised evaluation of all pesticides approved for use—a process mandated by the Food Quality Protection Act of 1996, but one that has proved woefully slow and full of loopholes.

Finally, pesticide risk must also be measured across generations. The class of chemicals known as endocrine disrupters move up the food chain, so that they are at their highest concentrations in breast tissue and are expressed through breast milk. This most perfect of nature's foods, then, becomes a carrier for potential risk to the next generation and beyond.

Endocrine disrupters mimic the hormones in the body and may be linked to hormone-related problems such as low sperm count, hormone-related cancers, and abnormal development of sexual organs.[1]

Pesticides were greeted as miracles when they first came on the world scene. But a lack of foresight and caution allowed these miracles to run amok and create irreversible damage. By understanding the mistakes that can happen when we blindly accept powerful new technologies, we can avoid similar errors in the future—as with, for instance, the genetic modification of foods.

CONQUERING MALARIA

Pesticides were first developed during the Second World War and quickly became a highly profitable global industry. Initially, these chemicals were enthusiastically greeted for their potential to control malaria, yellow fever, typhus, and other insect-borne diseases. In fact, the Nobel Prize in medicine was awarded in 1948 to the scientist who helped ascertain the ability of DDT to kill insects, although that same chemical later became synonymous with toxicity and was ultimately banned for use in this country in 1973 (though its residues persist today and it continues to be used in other countries).

Because mosquitoes carrying malaria caused devastating epidemics, it's easy to understand why a chemical that could efficiently destroy disease-carrying insects en masse, and which appeared to be much less toxic to humans than the alternatives in use at the time, looked like real progress. And because limiting or eliminating malaria was a factor in successful wartime military strategies, the government embraced the technology and assisted in facilitating its widespread use during World War II and its later adoption as a domestic agricultural technology in peacetime.

"When the choice to deploy DDT was made by military, health, and agricultural officials," writes John Wargo in *Our Children's Toxic Legacy: How Science and Law Fail to Protect Us from Pesticides*, "they could not have known that their fundamental logic of choosing near-term, certain benefits over uncertain long-term risks was to be adopted by the USDA as it licensed tens of thousands of products containing hundreds of newly discovered synthetic pesticides. This logic would support if not propel the agricultural chemical industry through its most rapid period of growth and innovation between 1945 and 1970."[2]

Following the war, the use of DDT became widespread, and we have disturbing photos from that time: DDT being sprayed in towns and on public beaches in the 1940s, with children playing in the chemical mist. "DDT provided clear and immediate benefits," Wargo writes. "It gave insecticides a health-promoting image, which in turn shaped the statutes and decision standards chosen to control pesticides since 1947. It has probably saved millions of children's lives, especially in tropical areas where insect-borne diseases still take their worst toll." Wargo's thoughtful and detailed book then goes on and "traces the changing image of pesticides from a technology that reduces risk to one that imposes it . . . as well as the management problems that result when knowledge of risk emerges long after government has licensed broad use of a hazardous technology."[3]

Evidence of toxicity did emerge, of course, far too late for those who experienced casual and intense exposure. And in a frustrating though probably foreseeable turn of events for the scientists who thought they'd conquered insect-borne diseases, insects bred for resistance to DDT fairly quickly. The cycle continues today, as powerful chemicals ultimately lead to resistant insects and more and different chemicals must be developed and applied.

RACHEL CARSON'S LEGACY

What has changed, to some extent, is our perception of these chemicals as harmless. With the publication of Rachel Carson's *Silent Spring* in 1962, a terrible warning was sounded: Modern insecticides were deadly, and wildlife and humans were not immune and would pay a heavy price for their uncontrolled use. Houghton Mifflin published a new edition of Carson's watershed work in 1994, with an introduction by then-Vice President Al Gore. "*Silent Spring* came as a cry in the wilderness, a deeply felt, thoroughly researched, and brilliantly written argument that changed the course of history," Gore wrote. "Without this book, the environmental movement might have been long delayed or never developed at all."[4]

Carson received a great deal of criticism when her passionate book was first published, however; she was called a hysteric and a throwback, resisting the modern worldview that humankind could control nature with impunity. But enough people paid attention to *Silent Spring* to seed the beginnings of a revolution. Carson's book remains powerful and relevant today and well worth reading for anyone who wants to understand how we got where we are today.

By the time Carson's warnings were being taken seriously, however, the pesticide industry was already a behemoth with a momentum that would prove hard to slow down. Vice President Gore, considered an environmentalist but by no means an extremist, wrote these words about the chemical industry in his 1994 commentary on *Silent Spring*: "For the most part, hardliners within the pesticide industry have succeeded in delaying the implementation of protective measures called for in *Silent Spring*."[5] Gore is describing the pesticide regulation system that governs the release of 5 to 6 billion pounds of insecticides, herbicides, fungicides, rodenticides, and other biocides *each year*. In fact, 5 billion pounds of DDT alone had been used worldwide by 1983.[6] Consider these somber words by John Wargo:

> Today, nearly 325 active pesticide ingredients are permitted for use on 675 different basic forms of food, and residues of these compounds are allowed by law to persist at the dinner table. Nearly one-third of these "food-use" pesticides are suspected of playing some role in causing cancer in laboratory animals, another one-third may disrupt the human nervous system, and still others are suspected of interfering with the endocrine system.[7]

Food-use pesticides are only part of the toxic burden borne today by both humans and the environment. Lawn and garden pesticides and fertilizers and indoor pest control products also contain toxic chemicals. Lumber and utility poles account for some of the greatest pesticide use, and chemical pest controls are widely used in our schools, homes, and office buildings.

BACK TO THE LAND

The post–*Silent Spring* era saw an uprising against 1950s values that took many forms. In the societal reckoning that followed President Kennedy's assassination and found its most passionate voice in the movement opposing the war in Vietnam, caring about "the ecology" and sharing in Carson's concerns became one of the signposts of a new way of thinking. Much has been written about all the ramifications—the successes and the failures—of the activist movements of the 1960s. If you're reading this book, it's likely that either you or your parents remember the '60s quite well and have some sense of how the cultural changes of that time have affected our lives today.

Diet and food production systems also came under the scrutiny of the counterculture movement of the 1960s and 1970s. Vegetarianism became more popular and health foods stores and cooperatives sprouted up in every community. As people searched for ways to be closer to nature, to simplify and purify their lives, growing food and doing it without toxic chemicals became part of many lives.

PLANTING ORGANIC SEEDS

Growing food without relying on chemicals was not entirely new. Throughout the development of a pesticide-based agriculture, there were still those who believed in soil fertility as the basis of sound agriculture. J. I. Rodale, a pioneer of organic farming methods, founded the Soil and Health Foundation in 1947 and created *Organic Farming and Gardening* magazine, which continues today as *Organic Gardening,* published by Rodale, Inc., in Pennsylvania.

J. I.'s Soil and Health Foundation became the Rodale Institute, which today is conducting important research about yield potential for organic farms. When pesticide advocates argue that organic farming can't feed the world, Rodale's research helps counter that hypothesis by showing yields of organic crops comparable to conventionally grown ones.

Another pioneer of sustainable agriculture was Rudolf Steiner, an Austrian philosopher whose work in the 1920s led to a method of agriculture known as biodynamic farming, which, according to the Biodynamic Farming and Gardening Association, based in San Francisco, "seeks to actively work with the health-giving forces of nature." According to the association, "It is the oldest non-chemical agricultural movement, predating the organic agriculture movement by some twenty years, and has now spread throughout the world."[8]

But for many years, the beliefs and philosophies of visionaries such as Rodale and Steiner were drowned out by the forward march of pesticides and chemical-based agriculture, which fast became the agribusiness we know today, with little or no "cultivation" at its heart. And when, by the 1960s, hippies and back-to-the-land advocates began growing food without chemicals, it took time for any of it to become formalized or to become commercially viable.

But the movement was under way. In spite of little in the way of consistency, convenience, and sometimes even hygiene, health and natural foods stores full of tofu, nuts, vegetables, and whole grains—plant-based foods—flourished. Those farming without chemicals began to discover and form real philosophies of ecological and sustainable farming that went beyond just the absence of chemicals to include principles of transparency (full documentation of ingredients and processes used), biodiversity, and attention to whole ecosystems. And produce labeled organic began to appear in health foods stores—often small and blemished, as cultivation methods were still somewhat unrefined, but still selling at premium prices and very much in demand as knowledge, and in some cases fear, about the risks of pesticides grew.

By the mid-1970s, the need for standardization of the organic label was becoming apparent. In 1974, Oregon passed a state law defining "organic," and a group of California farmers formed California Certified Organic Farmers (CCOF), the first U.S. organization to certify organic practices. Within its first decade, CCOF participated in writing a California state law defining organics, following Oregon's lead. Organic activists in Oregon, Washington, and California formed a loose affiliation called the Western Alliance.

Meanwhile, a trade organization formed in 1985 in Massachusetts called the Organic Food Production Association of North America, or OFPANA. (Today, OFPANA has become the Organic Trade Association, or OTA, and serves the needs of hundreds of member companies, large and small, engaged in organic production.)

Both OFPANA and the Western Alliance were working toward standards that would define organic language, practices, tools, transition periods, certification, and enforcement. The goal was to protect both farmers and consumers, shoring them up against potential fraud and exposure of inconsistencies by building rigor and integrity into the system. Consumers could look for the certified organic label and know that the money they might spend for organic foods was justified.

Organic standards and organic certification, it was thought, might also help arm the movement against those who wanted it to go away altogether. There were rumors that the FDA wanted an outright ban on the organic label. Regulation, for all its inherent complications and interference with farmer independence, seemed preferable to a ban.[9]

ALAR SPEEDS THINGS UP

And then, as with most stories of the late twentieth century, there was a pivotal media event that turned up the volume faster and higher than anyone expected. The Natural Resources Defense Council (NRDC), a nonprofit environmental advocacy organization based in New York, published a compelling report called "Intolerable Risk: Pesticides in Our Children's Food," in part documenting the dangers of daminozide, or Alar, a chemical growth regulator used primarily on apples, and the Environmental Protection Agency's failure to take timely action on those dangers.

In early 1989, a burst of high-profile media attention followed: *60 Minutes* broadcast a segment; the actress Meryl Streep aligned herself with NRDC's consumer arm in public statements opposing pesticide use; and *Time* and *Newsweek* put food safety on their magazine covers. The slogan "Don't panic, eat organic" was made for Alar, because panic was in the air. Suddenly, the public wanted organic foods, and for the first time, demand was far outstripping supply, even with premium prices on organically grown foods.[10]

This was indeed the beginning of organic agriculture's emergence from tiny niche market to real legitimacy in the larger food marketplace. But the likelihood of fraud in the organic world also increased vastly. The money to be made was growing exponentially. At the same time, more and more people were asking what organic meant, and some were looking more closely at the agricultural methods themselves. The term *organic* was sometimes being abused, and certification systems and governance were still undeveloped.

So the move toward legislation, both state and national, sped up in a rush to legitimize the movement for hordes of newly interested consumers. Within months of the Alar episode, organic factions were organizing further, trying to hold on to some power over standards in the face of opportunists hoping to cash in. New alliances formed, including the Organic Farmers Associations Council, the Organic Food Alliance, and a contingency of twenty-seven organizations that called themselves the Organic Working Group, led by Roger Blobaum, then at the Center for Science in the Public Interest.

Although many organic farmers, independent and innovative by nature, resisted the need for government approval of their methodology, this history helps explain why the drive toward legislation became absolutely necessary in the eyes of many. The organic movement eventually found its political friend and champion in Senator Patrick Leahy of Vermont, who agreed to sponsor a bill that would contain many of the provisions the organic community hoped for. His efforts in support of small farmers and his understanding of the concerns of organic advocates resulted in the passage of the Organic Foods Production Act of 1990 (OFPA), which mandated the development of a national set of standards for the organic label.

It was a critical step, but the fight was far from over. In late 2000, the USDA finally completed these national organic standards that may further change the landscape of the food production system and the organic movement. To create standards that even remotely supported the true tenets of organic agriculture required a massive consumer uprising over the first draft of standards. Yet it finally appears that consumers will have a standard they can understand and trust for any food labeled organic.

As the organic marketplace takes its place in its current state of commercial viability and growth, there has also been more and more research about the real effects and dangers of pesticides. Though organic foods have improved and their availability has increased a thousandfold, chemical-based agriculture continues to be the norm. And as the risks of these chemicals are further exposed, our exposure to them becomes an even greater concern. So the hope of everyone in the organic community is that national organic standards in practice will reflect both the letter and spirit of the organic community's long-standing principles.

SUMMARY

- Chemical pesticides and herbicides were initially used to kill disease-bearing insects and aid wartime strategies. These pesticides were greeted as miraculous, but problems with insect resistance and environmental damage became apparent fairly quickly.
- The organic movement grew in response to consumer demand for food grown without toxic chemicals in response to environmentalists striving to create a sustainable and ecological food production alternative.
- Organic standards have existed through a patchwork of certification programs and are now unified under one federal definition for foods grown with the organic label.

CHAPTER SIX

The National Organic Program and What It Means for Consumers

The passage of the Organic Foods Production Act of 1990 (OFPA) was a huge grassroots success. The bill mandated an advisory board, the National Organic Standards Board (NOSB), to be appointed within six months to write recommendations for a set of federally governed, nationally consistent standards for the organic label on foods. Though it would be eight years before an initial draft was released for public comment, and though that first draft would prove to be a dismal failure and force the USDA back to the drawing board, the very passage of OFPA, many believe, helped drive the continued growth of the organic marketplace. Organic commerce was growing at double-digit percentage rates, much faster than the more mature mainstream food industry.

OFPA accomplished this by enhancing the legitimacy of organic agriculture even prior to implementation of the law. Alar had opened the floodgates of the marketplace, and growers were responding to demand with more and better organic choices. Retailers were growing in size and number and quality of stores. And so it went. Business was good and getting better, which in turn may have helped some in government take organic more seriously.

Along the way, a patchwork of more than thirty state and private certifiers were acting as independent verifiers for organic production methods. This meant that a third-party organization, whether government-based, nonprofit, or private, would evaluate farms and food processors according to a given set of standards. Most certifiers used standards that were similar but not entirely uniform, and certification was not required by law in many places (though many stores required it to sell the product).

This patchwork of certifiers gave way to the contention, often seen in print, that the organic label had no meaning. Rarely would those making this assertion explain the availability of certified organic foods or the fact that many uncertified organic farmers were indeed following documented and carefully considered practices. In truth, if during the last twenty years you've been buying organic foods from a reputable grocer, buying certified organic foods, or buying directly from farmers at farmers markets or through community-supported agriculture, if it's been labeled organic, you've most likely been getting the real thing.

Still, there was a sense and in some ways a reality that national organic standards would make a difference to consumers, farmers, and the marketplace. The National Organic Standards Board undertook its work.

Despite years of organizational snafus and low funding, the National Organic Standards Board, made up (by law) of growers, retailers, scientists, food processors, consumers, and environmentalists, finally was able to write a set of recommendations and turn them in to the USDA. But when the USDA moved that proposed set of standards through requisite agencies and finally released them for public comment in December 1997, shockwaves went through the organic community.

The USDA's first proposal bore little resemblance to NOSB recommendations. The proposed rule was worse than anyone feared and would have destroyed the integrity of the organic label. Among other concerns, there were the so-called Big Three: The USDA stated that food irradiation, genetically modified organisms (GMOs), and sewage sludge as fertilizer would all be allowed in foods labeled organic. There were other problems as well, such as allowances for antibiotics in organic meat.

Organic advocates galvanized, gathered their forces, and waged war to prevent this proposal from becoming law, and they succeeded. The USDA received a record-breaking number of comments in response to a proposed law, assisted in part by the fairly new Internet technology that allowed them to receive comments electronically and also post them for viewing on-line. The USDA agreed to shelve the first draft of the standards and try again.

In March 1999, a second proposal was released for another round of public comment, which closed several months later. Secretary of Agriculture Dan Glickman had kept his word to prohibit inclusion of the Big Three (although there were some concerns about loopholes that might allow genetically modified foods in the organic production scheme in the future). Organic advocates were fairly satisfied with the bulk of the proposed standards and spent time closely examining the details, especially the way the standards would or would not help small farmers thrive, standards for organic livestock, specifics of materials that would or would not be allowed on certain crops or in certain production processes such as winemaking, and the aforementioned potential loopholes for transgenic technologies.

FINAL NATIONAL STANDARDS MARK A PIVOTAL MOMENT

In late December of 2000, the USDA released its final rule on standards for foods bearing the organic label in the United States. The tiny alternative industry had proven to be a significant movement that could now continue to grow, mature, and thrive on a national and international scale. The organic foods community, having fought Goliath on the first round of proposals, now finally had a standard it could largely accept and even applaud, as many organic foods companies and organizations did in press releases in that last week of 2000.

"I am proud to say that these are the strictest, most comprehensive organic standards in the world," said Secretary of Agriculture Glickman in a press conference marking the rule's release. "We said that we would deliver standards that could be embraced by farmers, industry, and consumers alike, and we have done exactly that." Glickman made note of the 275,603 comments that forced the first proposed organic rule to be redrawn—"more than one comment for every minute of the public comment period." The new and final standards, he said, "are the product of a full-throated public debate."[1]

In his remarks, Glickman also emphasized that "no food could be called organic if irradiation, sewage sludge, or genetic engineering was used in its production." Though he was about to leave his USDA post as a new administration prepared to enter the White House, Glickman closed by saying, "Now it's time to take the next steps—to fully embrace organic agriculture and give it a more prominent role in the farm policy of the twenty-first century."[2]

The scheduled eighteen-month implementation period meant that consumers could expect to see the "USDA Certified Organic" seal on foods in mid-2002.

The USDA's final rule, of course, couldn't please everyone in every way, and many organic advocates will be watching closely over the years to see how federal oversight of organic certification works in practice. The National Organic Standards Board continues to exist and to be responsible for making recommendations for changes and evolution of the standards to meet the needs of organic farmers, consumers, and the organic industry. In particular, I believe there will be those watching attentively to be sure that small farmers are not shut out of the system by the cost of the USDA-approved certification.

CONSUMER UNDERSTANDING, CONSUMER CONFIDENCE

It's been a long, strange trip for organic agriculture from its alternative beginnings to today's national standards. But what does it all mean for the average shopper? As I write this, the implementation process of these standards is just beginning, so there are many scenarios for the organic foods shopper of the future. But the hope and the intention of the national organic standards, as they've been written, is to offer a U.S. organic label of high integrity and consistent meaning in every state.

This means consumers can have confidence in the organic label. The details of the definition of organic production systems are now clear. For example, land on which organic crops are grown must be free from new chemical applications for three years before earning organic certification. All organic practices, including documentation and record-keeping, are articulated by the rule, which is hundreds of pages long.

The standards also specify consequences for mislabeling—a civil penalty of up to $10,000 for anyone who knowingly sells or labels as organic a product that is not produced and handled in accordance with the National Organic Program's regulations—and identifies steps that will be taken to remove certification from those who fail to meet the standards.

For many years, in many places, the meaning of the organic label was not clear or consistent. At the same time, consumers had and have strong ideas about what organic should mean, and have always wanted and deserved some assurance. Inconsistencies in organic labeling troubled many who felt that the often-higher prices charged for organic foods created a breeding ground for fraud. That argument has been silenced by national organic standards that, thanks to years of persistence, will maintain a level of integrity in organic agriculture.

The success of the organic movement, measured by rapid growth and mainstream acceptance, owes a debt not only to all its farmers and advocates but also to millions of individual consumers who embraced an alternative that gave more than the conventional food industry was offering. The availability of high-quality organic food meeting high organic standards is a testament to the power of the people to effect positive change, even in a world where it seems hard to beat the system. As a society, we are never again likely to abdicate all control over where our food comes from and how it is grown. The industrialized food system has had to take notice and will never be completely the same. Though it's important to keep fighting for sustainable systems that support health and community, the accomplishments of the organic movement to date are still something to be proud of.

USDA GUIDELINES FOR THE ORGANIC LABEL, EFFECTIVE MID-2002[3]

Under the provisions of the national organic standards, organic foods and foods made with organic ingredients can be distinguished by labeling in several ways:

- *100% Organic*
  These foods must contain, excluding water and salt, only organically produced ingredients.
- *Organic*
  These foods must consist of at least 95 percent organically produced ingredients, excluding water and salt.
- *Made with Organic Ingredients*
  Processed products that contain at least 70 percent organic ingredients can use the phrase "made with organic ingredients" and list up to three of the organic ingredients or food groups on the principal display panel.

  The USDA seal cannot be used on these packages, but the percentage of organic content and the certifier's seal or mark may be used.

  The nonorganic ingredients (30 percent or less) *may not* be genetically engineered or use other excluded methods or be irradiated or fertilized with sewage sludge.
- *Products made with less than 70 percent organic ingredients*
  These products can only identify organic ingredients in the ingredient statement and cannot use the USDA organic seal or a certifier's seal or mark.

While the national organic standards are extremely detailed, many consumers may not want to know every technical agricultural and regulatory aspect. In addition to the labeling guidelines above, here are a few more points that may be useful to shoppers:

- Farms and handling operations that sell less than $5,000 annually of organic products are exempt from certification but are expected to comply with the standards. Certification is not required for retailers and restaurants. As a consumer, though, look for and ask for "good organic handling practices"; for example, uncovered organic produce should not be commingled with conventional produce.
- The National Organic Program does not allow a "transitional

organic" label. Cropland must be free of chemical applications for a full three years before earning organic certification.
- Imported organic foods must meet the standards of the National Organic Program.
- The residue of pesticides allowed on organic foods is 5 percent of the Environmental Protection Agency's pesticide residue tolerance for conventionally grown foods.
- Organic livestock must be fed 100 percent organic feed (with a one-time allowance for 80 percent organic feed for dairy herd conversion) and organically raised animals may not be given growth hormones or antibiotics. Producers may not withhold treatment from a sick or injured animal, however; these animals are treated but may not be sold as organic. All organically raised animals must have access to the outdoors.
- The name and address of the certifying agent of the final product must be displayed on the information panel. This allows consumers to contact the agent for more information, if desired, about specific practices and methods.
- States have the option of developing their own organic program, which must be approved by the Secretary of Agriculture. State standards can be more restrictive than national standards.

SUMMARY

- National organic standards for organic production, under the oversight of the National Organic Program of the USDA, were finalized in late 2000 with implementation scheduled for mid-2002.
- The national standards prohibit not just synthetic pesticides,. herbicides, fungicides, and fertilizers, but genetic modification or transgenic technologies, irradiation, and the use of sewage sludge as fertilizer.
- The standards also prohibit antibiotics and growth hormones in

organically raised animals and require access to the outdoors for these animals.

- The standards are intended to help build the market for organic foods both domestically and internationally.
- For consumers, the standards offer the confidence inherent in a consistent and clear definition of "organic" and specific guidelines for labeling of organic products.

CHAPTER SEVEN

Label Stew: Making Sense of the Eco-labels

If the national organic standards will finally tell consumers exactly what the organic label means, how are we to interpret the rest of the labels that are out there that seem to want to be in the organic family? It's enough to make a shopper crazy—and confused. Alongside "certified organic" is a host of other labels implying an environmentally better choice: "pesticide-free," "unsprayed," "grown with Integrated Pest Management," "environmentally grown," and even that old standby, "natural." What's the difference, and what's a consumer to do?

While each label may have some validity, none means the same as "certified organic." If you've been reading this book, you have some understanding of what that means. It's a carefully documented and audited farming and food production system that, in principle, is founded on soil fertility, biodiversity, and an avoidance of synthetic chemicals, transgenic technologies, and hormones and antibiotics in livestock.

The rest of the labels that are popping up vary in credibility and substance. Consumers have made it clear that they're willing to pay somewhat more for products they believe to be less damaging or more beneficial to the environment and to human health. It's logical, then, that food producers are claiming that advantage any way they can—to give products and the companies themselves an appearance of environmental responsibility.

Sometimes it's true, and those companies deserve respect and support. In some cases, though, the buyer must beware. For example, what does "environmentally grown" mean? It could mean anything from food grown in any kind of soil—which would indeed be part of the environment—to a more formal program that actually has clear environmental components.

And what about "natural"? Legally, it means absolutely nothing. Any food company can label something as natural. When foods without chemical additives or preservatives became popular, the natural label got co-opted pretty fast. In fact, part of what drove the organic community to seek out national legal standards for organic was the fear that the same thing would happen all too quickly.[1] Now, fortunately, we're protected from that.

The burden of knowledge is on the consumer, however. Ask your grocer—or better yet, the growers themselves—a few pertinent questions. Read and consider the labels carefully. If you're paying higher prices for food with an "eco-label," make sure you feel informed about what it means. Don't make assumptions.

Mark Lipson, policy program director for the Organic Farming Research Foundation, offers these questions as an aid in judging an alternative or eco-label: Is it truthful? Does it actually mean something specific and tangible? Is it subject to transparent verification?[2]

WHAT DOES THE LABEL MEAN?

Dig a little to see how well defined the claimed practices are. For instance, unsprayed may mean that no sprayed chemicals are used, but are synthetic pesticides used in some other way? Is the soil free of pesticides from earlier crops? Are synthetic fertilizers or herbicides used? Is it a genetically modified crop? Is the crop unsprayed during trucking as well as on the farm?

The pesticide-free label is especially vague and probably impossible to uphold, since pesticides are everywhere—in our air, water, and soil. Even organic foods may not be completely pesticide-free—not because pesticides have been applied to them, but because of background contamination in the environment.[3] In fact, even DDT particles have been recently found in dirt on windowsills in countries where DDT has been banned for decades.[4] Either the chemical persisted in the environment or traveled literally thousands of miles, dispersed through the atmosphere.

Labels that say "GMO-free" (genetically modified organism-free) may also be misleading. Unless the product is certified organic, how does the company know? How often do they test? Most conventional food producers say they are unable to segregate genetically modified crops from those that are not modified. Testing is available, but expensive. McDonald's has publicly said that it asks its potato farmers not to grow from transgenic seeds. But what about the corn oil and soy lecithin in other products they sell?

One problem with the pesticide-free position is that it makes organic foods vulnerable to some misleading criticism by its opponents, which can be very powerful agribusiness interests. If you've seen headlines or claims that organic foods have pesticides—claims intending to discredit the organic industry—remember that pesticides are everywhere. Read the details and find out whether they're talking about fraud, residues from commingling organic and conventional produce in the store, or the unfortunate background contamination that exists everywhere.

HOW IS THE LABEL REGULATED?

In other words, who's watching? Is there an independent body verifying the claims? How frequently are checks or audits conducted on the farm? How long has the farm been using these practices? Is there any legal constraint on using the particular term, or can anyone put it on their label without consequence if the label is inaccurate? If there are legal limits on the term, what are they? The term *free-range* for chickens requires only that the pens have a door through which the chickens can (theoretically) leave or enter. It does not mean, as many assume, that the birds have open space on which to roam or that any other humane practices are necessarily in place.[5] It also doesn't mean they're not. You can't tell from the "free-range" designation alone. Only you, as a consumer, can insist on companies giving you enough information to make a confident choice according to your values.

Some well-established eco-labels are very legitimate, describing well-defined growing methods:

- *Biodynamic* describes an agricultural system based on the teachings of Rudolf Steiner, a philosopher with a spiritual bent, and is considered the oldest modern nonchemical form of farming. The Demeter Association certifies biodynamic farms internationally.

"More than simply avoiding chemicals, biodynamics seeks to actively work with the health-giving forces of nature," according to the Biodynamic Farming and Gardening Association.[6]

- *Transitional organic* is a term some private or state certifying agencies used in the past for farms using organic practices for less than three years (the time usually required to transition the soil from chemical farming). However, the national organic standards finalized in late 2000 do not define or permit this term on food labels.
- *Hydroponic* refers to a system of cultivation without soil that may or may not use synthetic chemicals. Plants are greenhouse-grown in water without soil, and all nutrients, synthetic or natural, are externally applied. The term simply describes the use of water or medium as a root base, rather than soil. Hydroponic is not the same as organic.
- *Integrated pest management (IPM)* is related more to landscape management for buildings, schools, offices, or golf courses than to food. It is an approach rather than a prescribed set of procedures. The approach seeks to minimize use of synthetic chemicals and to use them with minimal damage to the environment in conjunction with biological and cultural practices, such as choosing appropriate plants for the region. IPM is not a legally regulated label, but its practitioners keep records to monitor progress and challenges.[7]

Finally, what about organic foods that aren't certified? The new federal organic standards exempt small growers or producers from certification who sell less than $5,000 of organic product annually. Otherwise, food sold with the organic label, by law, requires certification with the implementation of USDA standards. Historically, some organic farmers have opted out of certification for a variety of reasons, from philosophical to economic, and a consumer's best strategy has been to know the farm and its systems. Otherwise, *caveat emptor.*

SUMMARY

- There are a number of eco-labels in the marketplace that are often mistaken for organic labels.
- These labels vary in their credibility, amount of information they offer, and levels of independent validation. Some are excellent informational marketing labels, some less so.
- Consumers should ask exactly what a label means and who's watching to make sure it's true, especially if prices are higher than for nonlabeled foods.

CHAPTER EIGHT

America's Disgrace:
Small Farms in Crisis

Small farms and rural communities are in crisis. The extent of this crisis is meaningful to anyone who buys and eats food. The survival of small farms does matter, whether farms and farmers are nearby or far away. Support of organic agriculture can be one way to help small farmers survive and thrive.

Today, the great majority of Americans live in cities or in suburban or "exurban" areas surrounding cities. In this setting, most of us like to imagine that small farms are still out there somewhere, bucolic and pristine. Yet few of us know a farmer or would even be able to name a nearby farm. We know that food is plentiful in the supermarkets, and few of us think beyond that about where that food comes from.

In fact, when asked where that food comes from, American children are likely to respond, "From the store." The concept of milk coming from a cow, peaches coming from a tree, or carrots growing under the ground is foreign at best. And when we do think about farms, we still, on some level, imagine them to be run by farmers, not computers; we don't think of them as massive food factories fueled by massive inputs of toxic chemicals.

But unfortunately, that's exactly what modern conventional farming looks like. One of its sad consequences is that its efficiencies and its relationship with government drive a harvest's value down so far that a farmer operating on a smaller scale cannot compete. According to USDA statistics, the number of farms has declined in this century from 32 million farmers living on farms between 1910 and 1920 to less than 2 million farms remaining today (not necessarily with farmers living on the land). Eighty-four percent of the average farm operator's household income comes from off-farm sources, and farmers are twice as likely to live in poverty as members of the general population.[1]

Those living in poverty, of course, are not the executives of the chemical companies and multinational food conglomerates that have appropriated every aspect of our food production system. Those claiming the necessity of this system are generally those who profit from it.

But consumers and our society as a whole lose a great deal when small farms are driven to near-extinction and when we accept the premise that an industrial food system means progress and improvement over a more diversified system with room for small farms and closely linked communities.

The loss of small farms is a tragedy for every consumer. The argument has been made that we can't fight progress—that the consolidation of farming into the hands of a few large corporations is an evolution that should make us proud. But allowing a few massive, centralized companies to own every aspect of the food production system—in what's called a "vertically integrated" system because every step of the farming system is an income stream for the corporation—puts all control of that system in the same hands. The interests of consumers and farmers become secondary at best to the increased profits and efficiencies of agribusiness.

THE PLIGHT OF SMALL FARMS

Small farms are a part of America's history and legacy. The West was settled by pioneers who dreamed of owning land and farming it. Today, making a good life from family farming is harder and harder to achieve. Unable to compete against corporate consolidation, farmers have been driven off the land in significant numbers.

The consequences of this trend are devastating to the farmers themselves and also to us all. Communities are diminished. We are removed from the source of our food. The quality of food has declined. And a way of life that was once viable and rewarding is lost to our sons and daughters as a meaningful option.

The United States is not the only country where small farmers are losing ground. Chemical agribusiness companies are multinational in their scope, and their goals tend to be the same everywhere: maximizing efficiency and profit at the expense of small farms, diversity, and community food security.[2] These companies tend to grow "gourmet" foods for export to richer countries, though they claim to be feeding the starving populations of the world.

In recent years, one of the most disturbing trends has been the consolidation of livestock farming and the increasingly inhumane treatment of animals in factory farming enterprises. Industrial agriculture packs maximum numbers of animals into minimal space, fostering disease and poor hygiene and generating toxic wastes with disposal problems that have an impact on the surrounding communities.[3] Increased disease in the pens means that animals need higher doses of antibiotics, which has led to public health concerns about human resistance to those same antibiotics because we are exposed to them through food and water. And factory-farmed animals are often given growth hormones to increase their growth and production—again to increase profits. Small farms used to be largely responsible for hog production in this country; today, the majority of hog production is controlled by very few companies, who reenact this scenario over and over. The same is true for almost every common form of livestock farming.[4]

Nobody wins except the chemical and agribusiness companies. Small farmers lose land, income, and hope; consumers lose in quality and control over the food supply; the animals lose through inhumane treatment; and communities lose because the life-generating small farm is replaced by a destructive and toxic profit center. And we can't assume that more food is being produced or that more people are being fed.

Turning Point, a coalition of more than eighty nonprofit organizations that favor democratic, localized, ecologically sound alternatives to current practices and policies, buys national media space to state the case against industrial agriculture. About small farms, they say, "*The situation is desperate.* Farming was once the most diversified and democratic economic sector in America, but today it's become among the most narrowly concentrated and anti-competitive. The effect on small farmers is to make them nearly extinct. It's America's great disgrace."[5]

HOW ORGANIC FARMS HELP SMALL FARMERS

Organic agriculture can be a lifeline for small farms and family farms that are otherwise unable to compete against factory-style agribusiness. Organic farmers currently can sell at competitive prices to a specialized market that so far hasn't reached the level of consolidation that industrial agriculture has. While it's true that mainstream food conglomerates like General Mills are buying organic foods companies, the size of organic farms on the average remains fairly small. These organic companies often have a tradition of working with small and family farms that we can only hope will continue. Still, it's said that 10 cents of every food dollar in America goes to Philip Morris (which owns Kraft and other large food businesses). That's a terrifying thought for many of us and one that I hope will encourage you to fight for opportunity for smaller farms and ranches.

The closer you go to the source, whether by shopping at farmers markets, through community-supported agriculture, at co-ops, or at stores and even restaurants committed to supporting small growers, the more likely it is that more of your food dollar will reach the farmer who grew the ingredients for your food.

WHO IS THE ORGANIC FARMER?

Once we recognize the value of small and family farms and face the many ways that our society, communities, and food production systems are failing them, the challenges and rewards of farming become more real. If agribusiness is efficient, anonymous, and faceless, then organic farming is agriculture with a human face, to use the words of Wes Jackson, founder of the Land Institute in Salina, Kansas, and author of *Becoming Native to This Place.*[6] But whose face is it?

The Organic Farming Research Foundation (OFRF), based in Santa Cruz, California, has conducted a biennial National Organic Farmers' Survey that helps answer that question. OFRF's purpose is "to foster the improvement and widespread adoption of organic farming practices." To that end, the nonprofit foundation has not only raised funds and disseminated grants for on-farm research, but led the fight for increased federal government funding for organic agriculture research. Since 1990, OFRF has raised over $1 million in support of organic farming research and information dissemination programs and has influenced decision makers at the federal level to pay more attention to the lack of such research there. The National Organic Farmer's Survey helps facilitate OFRF's mission by identifying specific activities and needs of organic farmers. The survey also helps the rest of us know a little bit more about that human face.

The staff at OFRF, including Executive Director Bob Scowcroft, Policy Program Analyst Mark Lipson, and Program Coordinator Erica Walz, who manages the survey, have reminded me that organic farmers have a great deal more in common with other farmers than they have differences. The two groups are by no means antagonists. Organic farmers are not all left-wing hippies; they fit no stereotype except, it seems, for some level of devotion to what they do—that is, to farm. They are farmers first.

In fact, many farmers—about one-fourth of OFRF survey respondents—have mixed organic and conventional operations. Many concerns of the agricultural community at large cross boundaries of method. And this country's crisis of small farms and rural communities is not limited to any one kind of agriculture. Organic farming does offer an alternative market and thus a potential lifeline for small farms, but only if consumers respect and insist on protection for that aspect of organic agriculture.

Survey respondents to OFRF's fourth survey and third national survey included 1,192 certified organic farmers in forty-four states. This is approximately a 25 percent return rate on 4,638 surveys sent out. The survey is extremely comprehensive, and anyone interested in a detailed analysis can purchase the 126-page full report from OFRF (see Resources). Here are some highlights of interest about the demographic profile—in other words, who the organic farmer is statistically. Some of these facts may be surprising.

- The average age of survey respondents is forty-seven and a half years.
- Twenty-five percent of respondents are under forty years of age.
- Fifty-six percent of respondents have college degrees.
- Eighteen percent have pursued graduate degrees.
- Twenty-one percent of respondents are female.
- Seventy-two percent of respondents are single-family sole proprietorships, and an additional 15 percent are family partnerships.
- Sixty-two percent of respondents farm full-time.
- Average acres farmed in total is 208; organic acreage averaged 140. Respondents farming less than 2 acres numbered 143, while those farming more than 1,000 acres numbered 50.
- Twenty-one percent of respondents have been farming for twenty-one to thirty years, while 19 percent are relatively new to farming, with one to five years of experience. Twenty-nine percent have been farming organically for six to ten years.
- The largest number of respondents, at 21 percent, grossed between $5,000 and $14,999 from farming in 1997. Twenty percent made less than $5,000. About 13 percent reported making $100,000 or more in gross income.

There is, in short, no single profile of an organic farmer, but most are small business operators or family businesses. They are well educated, both male and female, and many appear to have transitioned from conventional to organic farming. Gross income from farming is not high on the whole—these small businesses are not "making a killing" or doing this only for the money—and many must work off-farm. Their farming operations can be complex; they are certainly modern, and their approach is as scientific as it is conservationist.

Farmers are often described as independent and self-sufficient people with little tolerance for institutional interference. But in the case of the small organic farmer, that intolerance may come, in part, from a sense of futility as government and research institutions continue to give their attention to large, conventional farms. Laura Tourte, a member of the OFRF survey advisory committee, says, "The survey results, viewed in conjunction with other materials on organic agriculture, show that organic farmers are (and continue to be) trail blazers in that they have been able to make substantial gains in the areas of production and marketing with what they perceive to be very little support from public institutions and government agencies."[7]

The organic farmers I've met can't really be pigeonholed in any way at all, except that they get up earlier and work harder than anyone I've met in other occupations. They are farmers, and they are poets, writers, parents, artists, organizers, and more. When they're farming, they are not focusing on either the enormity of the task of feeding the world or the romance that the rest of us often attach to it. They're just working. But there is an inherent understanding of and love for the land that I believe is often expressed by saying less rather than more. Farmers love their farms. And they live with nature's uncertainties—and market uncertainties—in a way that requires that love to be deep and unconditional.[8]

The best way to learn who organic farmers are, of course, is to talk to them and buy from them.

SUMMARY

- Small farms, family farms, and rural communities are in crisis.
- Modern industrial agriculture, in a variety of ways, has forced small farmers off the land.
- Organic and sustainable agriculture practices can help by offering an alternative market to small farms.
- By buying "close to the source," you help farmers earn more of your food dollar; the farther from the source that dollar is spent, the more likely it will go to intermediaries and corporate profits.

CHAPTER NINE

More Than Fruits and Vegetables

Most of us think of produce when we think of organic foods. It's true that fresh produce is the crown jewel of the organic farmer and the purest form of the harvest. Organic tomatoes, lettuce, carrots, onions, apples, broccoli—these are the staples of the kitchen and an important part of any healthy diet.

But there's so much more that can be organically produced. The organic label is on processed foods, frozen foods, convenience foods, bulk foods, and pantry staples such as oils, vinegar, and spices. It's on dairy products, coffee, chocolate, wine, beer, juice, meat, and poultry. It's on cotton used in clothing, household linens, and personal care products.

Every one of these things originates on a farm that, if organic growing methods are used, protects and preserves the soil, promotes biodiversity, and does not rely on synthetic chemical fertilizers or pesticides. Every purchase of one of these products is a vote for the environment and for the consumer's right to know how the things we buy are produced. Beyond that, each of these products has its own story with its own environmental, health, and social dimensions.

ORGANIC DAIRY

Milk, cheese, sour cream, butter, yogurt—the whole dairy case is filled with organic products. For these products to be certified organic, farmers must use certified organic feed for the animals and avoid the use of antibiotics or growth hormones. (Animals are removed from the herd if antibiotics are used to treat an illness; they are not deprived of medicine.) Synthetic chemical additives and dyes are not used in these products.

Organic dairy farming really took off after Monsanto, a multinational agricultural chemical company based in St. Louis, Missouri, began widely marketing its genetically engineered rBGH, or recombinant bovine growth hormone (also known as bovine somatotropin, or BST, and by its brand name, Posilac) for use in dairy cows. The hormone increases milk production in cows, but other consequences can include increased infection in the animals, who are then treated with ever-increasing doses of antibiotics in a chemical cycle that seems both inhumane and dangerous.[1]

Above and beyond the problems caused by the rBGH itself, which have been underreported to the public, the subsequent increase in antibiotic use adds to an already existing problem of bacteria becoming resistant to these antibiotics. These drugs are then less effective in treating humans. The Washington, D.C.–based Center for Science in the Public Interest (CSPI) launched its Antibiotic-Resistance Project in 1999 to fight the overuse of human-use antibiotics in agriculture. Human-use antibiotics used as growth promoters and to treat animal disease, CSPI says, has led to increased rates of bacterial resistance among food-borne pathogens.[2]

Monsanto fought against, and continues to oppose, labeling of products in which rBGH is used, although their claims that rBGH presents no health risk to humans or cows have been repeatedly contested by a number of environmental and nutrition experts. But so far Monsanto has won its battle to sell the growth hormone to conventional dairies in the United States, though rBGH is banned in Canada and a moratorium has been effected in the European Union. Because large dairies commonly mix milk from a number of sources, one dairy farmer using rBGH affects the entire batch, and consumers have no way of knowing, in most states, which milk contains the hormone. Some states are now permitting dairies not using rBGH to label their products as such, after legal fights from companies including Organic Valley Cooperative and Stonyfield Farm.[3]

Organic dairy standards prohibit the use of rBGH as well as other hormones, genetically modified ingredients, and antibiotics. If you don't live in a state that allows "no rBGH" labeling (rBGH is also called BST), the organic label on dairy products—from milk to cheese to ice cream—is your only guarantee that the substance isn't present.

And if you've been convinced by the powerful Monsanto public relations machine that rBGH is safe, consider that the hormone causes milk to have elevated levels of another hormone known as insulin-like growth factor (IGF-1). Studies at the University of Illinois and elsewhere suggest that increased levels of IGF-1 in humans may increase the risk of breast and colon cancer.[4]

There's very little about rBGH or, for that matter, other conventional dairy farming practices that benefits either cows or small farmers. Organic dairy products are now widely available and can help make for happier cows and healthier humans.

ORGANIC MEATS AND POULTRY

Although many ranchers were raising beef cattle and chicken organically according to private certifiers' standards, the USDA didn't allow an organic label on meat and poultry until 1999.[5] These meats, then, are welcome additions to the long list of organic food products. Although not everyone chooses to eat meat, those who do now have an alternative to factory-farmed beef, pork, chicken, and turkey.

Organic meat means that the herds are fed certified organic feed and graze on organic land and that the animals are treated humanely. No antibiotics are allowed in animals raised organically; animals who get sick and require antibiotics for treatment are removed from the herd. In conventional ranching, antibiotics are widely used and have come under increased scrutiny for their impact on human health.

Organic ranching practices also forbid the use of growth hormones in animals, another widespread practice in the conventional ranching industry that may have negative implications for human health.

ORGANIC COTTON

The fabric that so many of us choose and love for its natural characteristics can be more environmentally costly than the polyester we might disdain. Cotton is one of the most heavily sprayed crops in the United States, and conventional cotton production uses some of the most toxic and persistent pesticides available.[6] It's also fast becoming one of the major genetically engineered crops.[7]

Organic cotton, on the other hand, fulfills all the promise of natural fibers. It has comparatively little environmental impact and is as breathable and soft as we expect cotton to be. Yet it's still hard for a lot of people to see the value of organic cotton. If it doesn't go into our bodies, they reason, what difference does it make how it's grown? It takes a real understanding of the environmental benefits of organic agriculture, as well as a recognition of the impact of agriculture on our communities and planet, to see that organic cotton is an important choice.

And in fact, some by-products of cotton do end up in our mouths. Cottonseed oil is a common ingredient in many foods, and cottonseed is used in animal feed. Organic cotton fiber itself makes clothing, household linens including sheets and towels, infant clothes and diapers, personal care and grooming products, and paper.

Some apparel companies have pioneered broad use of organic cotton and helped create a market for the crop. They've also shown that organic cotton clothing can be both stylish and practical. For example, since 1996, outdoor clothing manufacturer Patagonia has used only organic cotton in its manufacturing after an analysis showed that 100 percent cotton, conventionally grown, was the most environmentally costly of all the fibers the company was using when complete costs were accounted for. Patagonia also sells organic cotton T-shirt blanks for other individuals or companies to use to create their own designs. And the company has become a leader in communicating the necessity and importance of organic cotton to other sport and apparel companies, setting a high standard for others to aspire to.

Organic cotton has also been a boon to sufferers of environmental allergies and to parents of newborns trying to create a relatively toxin-free environment for vulnerable infants. And though organic cotton clothing once seemed limited to the blandest colors and only "hippie" styles, savvy designers have stepped up to the plate, making sophisticated clothing in rich colors, such as the suits and coats made by New York's HealthyEverything.com. Organic fabrics and yarns are available for the home sewer and knitter too. Two good resources for organic cotton companies are *Care*

What You Wear: A Consumer's Guide to Organic Cotton, published by Mothers & Others for a Livable Planet, and the Organic Trade Association's *Organic Fiber Directory* (see Resources).

ORGANIC COFFEE

The satisfying brew that starts your day—or the mocha almond cappuccino at your favorite coffeehouse—is the final link in a long chain of agriculture, industry, and socioeconomic activity. The beans you buy have an impact on the global environment. And because most coffee is grown in developing countries, the coffee industry is also a stage for issues of fair trade, social justice, and community health.

Coffee is a stimulant, and opinions vary on how much coffee is safe to drink. Some health professionals think it's safe in moderation and may even have some beneficial effects; others think it can be detrimental for some aspects of health and may be a special concern for pregnant women. Adults should make a thoughtful choice with their health practitioners about caffeine and its effects on the body. If you choose to drink coffee, organic coffee may be a better choice for you as well as for the environment; chemically grown coffees have been shown to retain pesticide residues, sometimes even after roasting, including such toxic chemicals as DDT, now banned in this country but still in use elsewhere in the world.[8]

Those same pesticides, when applied on the farm, can have a very serious and sometimes fatal effect on the health of coffee plantation workers and their families. Workers in other countries use these toxic chemicals with extremely high exposure and often without regulation, and they and their families suffer.

In the tropical climates where coffee beans are grown, the factory farming methods that have evolved are creating environmental changes in these sensitive bioregions that may have global consequences. Chemical farming utterly dismantles the subtle yet strong balance that nature has devised. Coffee grows well in an ecosystem that includes trees of other kinds to provide a shade canopy, and within that simple relationship is a complex ecological system. Each part of the system helps the others thrive, and chemicals are unnecessary. There are biological pest controls and neighboring crops that preserve soil health, and the shade canopy itself is home to many species of songbirds.

Environmental problems began when, in an effort to grow coffee where it does not naturally grow, the industry cultivated a coffee plant that grows in sun. These "sun coffee plants" need a great deal of chemical treatment, in part because the biological pest controls that work so well in shade do not exist. The sun coffee plants are largely monocropped, or grown without beneficial neighboring crops or field rotation. Yet this unnatural "hothouse" version of a coffee plantation has meant profit for large companies, so they continue to proliferate, driving out the smaller, sustainable, shade-grown coffee farms. As these small farms fail, so do the numerous species they house—the songbirds, the shade plants, and the very human farm families who cannot compete with the large chemical farms.[9]

Along with healthy farm families, organic practices protect the fertility and quality of the soil and the integrity of the water supply in surrounding areas. Chemical farming and the attendant practice of monocropping depletes the soil, necessitating synthetic fertilizers and ever more pesticides and herbicides. Chemicals run off into the water supply and can be a major source of pollution. Eventually, the scavenged land is fallow and may remain so for many years before it can sustain life again.

Once harvested, coffee is a volatile commodity, and right now prices are high. Yet many organically grown beans are competitive in price with other good-quality roasts. There are many responsible roasters offering certified organic beans. Labels such as "shade-grown" or "sustainably harvested" are not the equivalent of organic, and you should ask the sellers exactly how they're defining these terms and what kind of independent verification exists. Organic certification is your best guarantee that your beans are grown in full compliance with organic standards.[10]

Organic methods should also include a commitment to principles of diversity and community. Organic coffee companies in particular have had to look carefully at issues of social justice, Third World development, and labor practices. A number of them give back time and money to their source communities and workers, for whom health, well-being, and education have been scarce. Look for information about these programs in brochures and on labels.

Organic coffee helps us to renew important connections, to deepen our understanding of ecological systems and how they are inexorably linked to the double espressos we drink in urban coffee bars. In some cases, the failures and successes of modern agriculture have taught us how little we fully understand nature's networks and the consequences of the powerful technologies we unleash. Left to her own devices, nature creates a lush tropical symphony in coffee-growing regions. Controlled by chemicals, these critical bioregions die a slow death. So make that cup organic!

ORGANIC CHOCOLATE

The many varieties of incredibly delicious organic chocolate, from chocolate bars to hot cocoa to baking chocolate, attest to organic foods' evolution into some of the very finest (some would say decadent) food choices available today. Once again, chocolate consumption is a personal choice. Some of us live for good chocolate, and now we can enjoy it while also supporting all of organic agriculture's environmental and social benefits.

Like coffee beans, cacao beans, from which chocolate is made, are grown primarily in developing countries within the context of a complex tropical ecosystem. And like coffee beans, cacao beans grow best with a natural shade canopy above them. This natural shelter is also home to migratory songbirds; one of the most poignant consequences of intensive chemical farming and monocropping of coffee and cacao trees in sunlight is the destruction or loss of these bird habitats due to deforestation.

The Smithsonian Migratory Bird Center of the Smithsonian Institution helps educate consumers about the connection between how coffee and chocolate are grown and the migratory birds that visit our backyards in the United States. When grown traditionally or organically, the shade canopy that protects the coffee and cacao trees also supports more forest-dependent migratory birds than any other agricultural habitat, the center says.

Of course, organic cacao farming also has real benefits for humans as well as for a vast diversity of other species that also thrive in the shaded rain forest canopies of organic farms. And as with other forms of organic farming, small farmers have the opportunity to sell their goods at a fair market price without being shut out by large companies using high-efficiency techniques at the expense of other values.

It's also worth noting that many chocolate and candy products contain soy lecithin, a soy product that, in conventional manufacturing, now has a very good chance of being made from genetically engineered soybeans. Genetic modification is not allowed in organic production, and an organic chocolate bar should use soy lecithin as an ingredient only if it is produced from non–genetically modified (and otherwise organic) soy. Organic sugar, an ingredient often found in organic chocolate products, also has huge environmental benefits over conventional sugar.

Because of the connection to the rain forest and tropical regions, many organic chocolate manufacturers donate some percentage of profits to communities and environmental projects in these regions. In the case of Newman's Own Organics, a division of Newman's Own, all profits from all their chocolate bars (including chocolate-covered peanut butter cups) are donated to social causes, just as the parent company does with profits from its popcorn, salad dressings, and spaghetti sauces. Look, too, for other organic chocolate companies with strong environmental and social programs to sweeten your purchases even more.

ORGANIC WINE

"The vine makes the true savor of the earth intelligible to man. It senses, then expresses, in its clusters of fruit the secrets of the soil," said French writer Colette. She was referring to the grapevine, of course, expressing the soil's secrets as fine wine. Yet if that soil is contaminated with chemicals, its "secrets" may be compromised and even harmful. But vineyards using organic growing methods are re-creating the wine industry as a celebration of artisanship and environmentalism and passing this spirit on to consumers as excellent wines that are wholly compatible with the finest foods.

As Colette artfully expressed, good soil is essential to good wine grapes; it's the subtleties and richness of the soil in a vineyard that create the hints of vanilla, smoke, berries, herbs, or other essences. Because the heart of organic agriculture is the cultivation of good soil and natural ecosystems that are appropriate to region and climate, organic wine should and, in the hands of a good winemaker, does reflect the richness of the land. Organic wines, or wines made from organically grown grapes, are competitive in taste, quality, and price with other fine wines.

It's important to note a distinction here. Some organic wines are processed without sulfites, a preservative that can improve the chances of wine aging well but that can also stimulate allergic responses, sometimes severe, in sensitive individuals. Thus, some vineyards choose to make an all-organic wine with no sulfites added other than the minute amount that may naturally occur in the winemaking process. Others grow the grapes organically, generating all the benefits of organic agriculture, but use a minimal amount of sulfites in the wine. The label will tell you if sulfites have been added:

- Wine labeled "made from organically grown grapes" assures you that all the agricultural principles of organics have been met, but processing may include additives, usually sulfur dioxide in amounts under 100 parts per million (ppm), well below conventional wine limits of 350 sulfite ppm.
- Wine labeled "organic wine" means that all organic standards are met in growing and processing. For clarity, wineries not using sulfites may specify "no sulfites added."
- All wine, no matter how the grapes are grown, with more than 10 ppm sulfites must be labeled as "containing sulfites." Naturally occurring sulfites usually range from 8 to 10 ppm, so even wine without *added* sulfites may have this verbiage on the label.
- If you have a favorite wine with no reference to organic practices on the label, call the winery and ask how their grapes are grown. Many wineries have adopted commendable sustainable and/or organic practices or are making the transition to organic, but choose not to put it on the label.

ORGANIC CORNUCOPIA

Organic selections go on and on. There are organic vinegars and olive oils, as beautiful and flavorful as fine wines, and organic olives, nuts, and cheeses for gourmands. Organic beer such as the Wolaver's brand is tasty and free of contamination from preservatives or fungicides used on hops for beer. Organic grains, cereals, pasta, and breads come in every imaginable form. In fact, artisan bread making is another revived culinary art that brings the hand of the maker back into the food system.

There are organic baby foods and many foods that children especially like and eat a lot of, such as the plump raisins grown at Pavich Family Farm. Children's juice drinks, macaroni and cheese packages, and cereals all cater to their tastes.

Organic snacks and convenience foods abound. Not everyone likes to see the organic food system mirror the conventional system with highly processed and packaged foods, even if they're processed to organic standards. It's well worth thinking about, though a lot of these products are pretty hard to resist. Nonetheless, there's something to be said for fresh whole foods close to their original state.

Organic tomato products are delicious. The tomato is undoubtedly one of the foods that has suffered most with conventional farming and storage methods, and for many of us, the first taste of a real organic tomato is an epiphany. That same flavor translates into pasta sauces, juice, and even Bloody Mary mix.

SUMMARY

- Fresh produce is the jewel in the crown of organic foods, but don't stop there. Expand your organic experience to include dairy products, meat and poultry, cereal, baby foods, grains and pasta, wine and beer, and cotton products, from personal care to clothing.

CHAPTER TEN
Where to Buy Organic Foods

Where can you find all these organic foods? These days, almost anywhere. Natural and organic foods are no longer found only in gourmet food havens like Berkeley or in college towns like Cambridge or in posh cities like Boulder or Austin. The health foods stores of old have evolved into modern independent markets or chain-style supermarkets; some natural foods co-ops still thrive, and the co-op concept helps neighborhoods unite to buy in bulk; conventional supermarkets are offering more and more organic choices; farmers markets proliferate, bringing a closer connection to the farmer and the freshest food available; and community-supported agriculture (CSA) programs offer a true sense of ownership and participation in farming. Finally, though grocery shopping via the Internet hasn't grown as fast as some forms of e-commerce, there's a lot of organic food on the Web.

Each venue for purchasing organic foods has its benefits and drawbacks. Fortunately, shoppers can avail themselves of all the different ways to support organics. Whenever possible, look for sources as close as possible to the original grower of the food. While you can't always purchase direct from the farmer, you can in every instance ask purveyors to support local farmers and identify the source of fresh produce, and you can support manufacturers of processed foods that buy ingredients from small and local farmers.

Here's a look at the different avenues for purchasing organic foods.

NATURAL FOODS SUPERMARKETS

On the plus side, natural foods supermarkets offer amazing selection, variety, and usually high quality and consistency. On the negative side, prices tend to be high, and as chains grow, there is increasing centralization rather than a regional/community base.

For most Americans, natural foods stores are one logical place to buy organic foods. There are thousands of such stores; they vary in size and sophistication, but they're almost all very different from the health foods stores of the 1960s and 1970s. Yet those early stores—filled with character, community, and passion—helped seed a movement that has grown beyond the expectations of anyone you'd have asked back then. Those stores provided the first marketplace for organic foods, with a vision of creating a food system that was a real alternative to the increasingly monotonous, big-box conventional supermarkets that were being controlled by fewer and larger corporations.

In the wake of those small, alternative health foods stores, a few entrepreneurs around the country had an inspiration. What if a grocery store could specialize in natural and whole foods, yet offer a full range of products and services and a more sophisticated ambiance? What if the stores were large, well lit, with the wide aisles of conventional supermarkets, but with clear standards that fully informed the consumer? And what if these same stores could also be cornerstones of the community instead of endless clones of the same anonymous box? That was the intention of the people who started companies such as Mrs. Gooch's, Alfalfa's, Wild Oats Market, Whole Foods Market, and Bread & Circus.

The success of these stores started waves of consolidation. Today, Whole Foods Market and Wild Oats are public companies with one-hundred-plus stores, having purchased many smaller stores and chains. They're building large "supernatural" markets with vast selection and a full range of services, including prepared foods, delis, full meat counters, bakeries, and more. The early standards of stores like Mrs. Gooch's, which originally excluded sugar, coffee, white flour, and meat, have given way to standards that embrace the gourmet as well as the natural foods shopper.

If you have one of these natural supermarkets in your community, you know they have a lot to offer. Their increasing size and fast pace of growth have also meant trade-offs, however; the barriers to small or local growers and manufacturers are higher, for example. It's often hard for smaller, locally owned natural foods stores to compete when one of these chain natural foods markets enters the neighborhood. And some feel that the level of business consolidation has led to a weakening of the community principles that originally guided these companies. It also must be noted that prices are likely to be as high or higher here than at any other venue for purchasing natural foods; those who think they can't afford to buy organic foods are likely to be using these stores as a measure.

A note of caution: Don't make the mistake of thinking that everything in these stores is *organic.* Generally, these chains use high standards that prohibit use of synthetic chemical additives in all items, but as we've seen, that's not the same as certified organic. In the produce department, you're likely to find conventionally grown foods, organically grown foods, and sometimes foods from farms in the three-year transition period required for organic certification. Responsible markets label these different choices clearly and should take great care to separate organic foods from conventional to prevent contamination.

INDEPENDENT NATURAL FOODS RETAILERS

On the plus side, independent natural foods retailers are usually locally owned, with a history of commitment to natural foods and to community. On the negative side, these retailers may not have the consistency of supply and convenience of larger natural foods stores, and there may be only a minimal selection of body care and household products.

There are still independent natural foods stores that have resisted merging with one of the large chains. Supporting locally owned businesses can be very important to the health of the community at large. These stores can also offer a unique character that chain stores, for all their advantages, cannot. Furthermore, independent natural foods stores can still provide opportunities to small and local growers and manufacturers and are often willing to work with them where larger stores cannot or will not.

Many independent retailers offer a selection that rivals that of the natural foods chain supermarkets and have long-standing relationships with their communities. It's possible you'll find a greater level of personal attention and service, though there may be trade-offs in convenience. Most retailers believe that there's room for both the big "supernaturals" and the independent stores; in fact, some communities thought to be saturated with natural foods shopping sites have proved that they can sustain many different kinds of stores. Look for those that make shopping enjoyable, that have well-educated, knowledgeable, and enthusiastic staff, and that really seem to understand and stand behind their stated principles, whatever the size of the store.

NATURAL FOODS COOPERATIVES

On the positive side, you can, as a co-op member, participate in many store decisions and in its success; you're participating in a real community-driven food system. And co-ops often have strong relationships with local suppliers. However, the biggest benefits of the co-op arrangement go to those who are active and willing to put in some effort, rather than the passive shopper.

The co-op model was vital to the success of the organic movement. In a cooperative buying system, consumers organize to buy bulk foods at whole-sale prices, and each person participates in the distribution process by working for the co-op or buying a membership, or both, to earn lower prices. The exact system varies with the co-op, of course, since its very nature is to serve the community and eliminate wholesalers and other intermediaries.

Though not as popular as they were in more activist decades, some natural foods co-ops are venerable and established with hugely loyal memberships. Like natural foods retailers, co-ops have grown in sophistication and selection, and the old stereotypes of musty, messy, closet-size stores are outdated.

Size isn't necessarily an indication of co-op success, but the potential for growth in these community-owned businesses may surprise you. The eight stores of Pacific Consumer Co-op, or PCC, in the Seattle area are collectively owned by the organization's forty thousand members. The Davis Food Co-op in Davis, California, has five thousand members; anyone can shop at the beautiful, member-owned store, with price differentiation for members and nonmembers.

Community involvement and interests are paramount to the co-op framework. If you like the idea of sharing in the ownership and decision-making process for your food source, and if you want to have a stronger voice and a sense of shared purpose, look for a co-op in your area—or start one.[1]

CONVENTIONAL SUPERMARKETS

On the positive side, conventional supermarkets offer all the convenience of modern "big-box" shopping for conventional and crossover items at moderate prices, and they are often a good place to pick up organic snack foods, frozen foods, and canned goods. On the negative side, most conventional supermarkets in the United States still offer limited selection, especially in produce; limited staff knowledge; and much of the selection comes from the largest organic companies or from those owned by multinational companies, such as General Mills or Kraft (which is in turn owned by Philip Morris).

Many conventional supermarkets are increasing their selection of natural and organic foods. It's a trend that is likely to continue as the organic market grows, as national standards for the organic label are implemented, and as consolidation into the food industry continues, putting more control over organic foods into the hands of bigger companies.

However, many of these stores are not prepared to be attentive to organic foods in the way that natural foods stores must be. The organic choices may be put in a small section in the back of the store; and with poor display may come poor turnover, reducing the quality of the selection.

On the other hand, some stores, such as the Pratt supermarket chain in Oklahoma, have made a real commitment to organic foods and understand how to showcase them as a premier choice rather than a choice that seems a bit out of place, as it does in many supermarkets. You can count yourself lucky if you have one of these "crossover" stores, where you can buy conventional necessities you may prefer and also find a full selection of organic foods and a knowledgeable staff.

If the fresh organic produce selection in conventional stores may sometimes disappoint, usually these stores are good places to find organic canned tomatoes, frozen vegetable burgers, organic cereals, crackers, and snacks, and other organic foods from some of the larger manufacturers at a good price. Some organic dairies have also made good inroads into the conventional markets.

Supermarkets in Europe may lead American supermarkets to increase their commitment to organic foods. The British chain of about eight hundred supermarkets called Iceland announced in 2000 that they were converting all of their offerings (primarily frozen foods) to organic.[2] To do so, they say they're making commitments to farmers and distributors that may have tremendous implications for global organic foods commerce.

In fact, European consumers are in love with organic foods. Both organic farm acreage and organic food sales are growing astronomically, in part because Europeans have so strongly rejected genetic engineering in the food supply. That and other food safety concerns have made organic foods wildly popular and widely available.[3]

FARMERS MARKETS AND CSA FARMS

On the positive side, when you buy from a farmers market or CSA farm, you're buying direct from the farmer. In many ways, this is the best possible choice whenever it's possible to make it. On the negative side, there are seasonal limitations.

Farmers markets and community-supported agriculture, or CSA programs, offer the strongest connection to the source of your food short of growing it yourself. They are wonderful ways to explore the world of real, seasonal, fresh food.

Though there are more and more stores of every kind offering organic foods, the most rewarding way to buy organics is direct from farmers. These alternative avenues of distribution allow farmers to bypass intermediaries and brokers, which can be helpful to small farmers trying to thrive.

There are also benefits for consumers. Buying straight from the farmer offers freshness and, sometimes, cost savings. But our connection to farmers is also important to our sense of community and conservation. Until we understand anew where our food comes from and our vital need to restore, preserve, and protect farmland and small farmers, rural communities, and our right to know how food is grown and produced, our health and sustainability as a society is at risk. Buying food from the people who grow it is one step in the process of renewing our sense of the source of our food.

Farmers Markets

If you have ever shopped in the relaxed community setting of an old-fashioned outdoor market, with the freshest vegetables, fruits, and flowers sold by the people who grow them, then you know the feeling of shopping at a farmers market. It's a far cry from supermarket shopping, where fluorescent lights, long lines, and food from who-knows-where is the order of the day. Supermarkets offer convenience, of course, and that has its value. But the pleasures of an outdoor market go far beyond convenience.

Farmers markets are proliferating today, with hundreds of regularly scheduled seasonal open-air markets in cities and towns everywhere. In Boulder, where I live, the downtown market is typical of today's farmers market; open every Wednesday and Saturday from late spring through early fall, local farmers sell the harvest of this region.

Right now, in August, that means Colorado peaches, nectarines, and cherries, Rocky Ford cantaloupe, sweet corn, chili peppers of every color and level of heat, cut herbs and herb plants, greens, flowers, deep purple

Japanese eggplants against a background of golden sunflowers, and more. Next month squash and pumpkins will be more prevalent, then apples and also huge roasters filling the air with the scent of roasting chilies that can be frozen for the winter. With regular visits to the market, the patterns of the local growing season become clearer and more meaningful.

In California, with a long growing season and varied climate, the selection at farmers markets can be truly amazing: organic heirloom fruits and vegetables; every variety of lettuce; yellow, orange, and red cherry tomatoes; sugar snap peas—the choices change with the season. In the East, Jersey tomatoes and Maine blueberries are at their best. Some of the finest chefs, from New York to San Francisco, make menu choices only after going through the markets to see what's available, what's fresh, what is the very best of that moment in that place. Instead of importing ingredients from far away, the freshness of regional flavors becomes the palette for the evening's creations.

Alice Waters, the famed founder and chef of Chez Panisse in Berkeley, California, turned the gourmet world upside down when she first hired a special "forager" who would seek out the finest, freshest, local ingredients. The growing popularity of farmers markets lets each of us be a forager and experience food and seasonality in a different way. Instead of buying food to fit a recipe, creative cooking can suggest itself to us through the ingredients at hand.

There doesn't have to be anything profound or romantic about farmers markets. They make perfect sense as part of every community, and it would be wonderful to be able to take something as straightforward as buying food from farmers utterly for granted. But as things stand, the true beauty of farmers markets is the rare possibility of real connection between grower and eater. It's what the modern food system has taken from us, an invisible dimension that really does make the food itself different.

Not every farmers market restricts sellers to organic foods; the Boulder market, for example, has vendors with signs proudly proclaiming that they're certified organic, but other vendors there use other farming methods. In every case, the growers are small farms who, when asked, can tell you exactly what methods they use, give you samples of their harvest, and tell you why the apple crop will be late this year and the squash will be exceptionally sweet and flavorful.

While certified organic foods may be your best choice for all the many reasons outlined in this book, you have the unique opportunity at market to talk to the farmer and make choices accordingly. Buying from transitional organic farmers helps support and vindicate their choice to go organic. Buying from farms that limit pesticide use still supports your local economy and gives you the chance to encourage these farms to make the conversion to organic production, if that's what you believe in. And in every case, you can reeducate yourself to think of seasonal and locally grown foods as a valuable part of your diet.

The point is that you can find out how your food is grown and what's been used on it; it doesn't have to be a mystery or a guess. What you ingest then becomes your choice rather than the choice of a chemical company, a multinational corporation, or government standards that may not be adequate.

If you're lucky enough to have a farmers market in your community, make it a regular part of your life. Many markets are more like weekly or twice-weekly festivals, with crafts for sale, prepared foods, beverages, music, and other events. And for serious food shoppers, many markets now have Web sites that can give you a preview of what will be available. The Boulder County market Web site, for instance, has recipes, a crop calendar, regulations for sellers, schedules, special events such as farm tours, and links to farm Web sites.

Markets also tend to reflect the community in which they're held, which is as it should be. But if the flavor of a particular market doesn't suit you, there's probably another not too far away. Here in Boulder County, some of my friends prefer the more down-home approach and diversity of a nearby market in the town of Longmont to the somewhat more sanitized and crowded "gourmet" market in downtown Boulder. When nearby markets are held on different days of the week, the truly devoted market enthusiast can visit them all. Fortunately, farmers markets are proliferating, so there's an opportunity to explore all the options in a region. (See Resources to help locate markets in your community.)

Community-Supported Agriculture

Visits to farmers markets, farm tours, and a growing awareness of where food comes from might inspire you to take the next step and join a farm that practices community-supported agriculture (CSA).

The community-supported agriculture movement began in the 1960s in Japan, where consumers concerned about dwindling farmland banded together to help guarantee, a season at a time, that growers would have buyers for the harvest. Today there are about a thousand community-supported farms in North America, according to the Center for Integrated Agricultural Systems, based at the University of Wisconsin in Madison.[4]

CSA farms can be large or small, offering provisions from seasonal organic vegetables to poultry, meat, and eggs. The common thread is a partnership between farm and community. Shareholders, or members, purchase a stake in the farm at the beginning of the growing season, giving the grower capital to run the farm. Depending on the farm and the length of the growing season, shares can cost a few hundred dollars or more; singles or small families might split a share with neighbors.

In return for this initial investment, as crops are harvested, each shareholder receives a portion of the farm's yield. These products might be delivered weekly to members at a pickup location, or shareholders can visit the farm to pick up allotments. As the season progresses, crops change; an early-spring box might hold cool-weather crops such as lettuce and asparagus, while late summer would bring a bounty of tomatoes, peppers, and zucchini. Farmers often include herbs and flowers and provide recipes, newsletters, and other educational materials along with the harvest.

By paying in advance for a full season of produce or other foods, members are likely to save money; studies comparing a CSA shareholder's seasonal take with equivalent produce at retail shows savings in every instance, sometimes significantly so, for CSA members.[5] What's more, produce usually gets in the hands of CSA members within a day of picking, compared to several days for even the freshest produce in many retail stores.

To get the most out of CSA membership, it helps to have a sense of adventure and improvisation in terms of what you'll be eating. While a crop calendar for your region and your CSA farm offers general guidelines about which foods will be in your member's box and when, you'll also experience firsthand the occasional vagaries of small-scale farming. You may also receive produce you wouldn't normally buy, whether it's an unusual variety of heirloom tomato or fruits and vegetables not ordinarily part of your family's diet.

As a CSA member, you share in both the risks and rewards of farming. A season of harsh weather will affect members' purchase in very real ways, with less variety or abundance, while a good year will reward members with the very best the farm has to offer. It's a long-term partnership that asks for a greater and different kind of involvement than simply going to the store and buying shrink-wrapped packages of food. While most of us hear about farmers suffering in drought years or losing crops to infestations, flooding, or heat, we rarely experience these things directly. Joining a CSA offers an opportunity to enjoy a deep connection to farming and foods but also to recognize the reality of what it takes to bring good food to the table and to embrace human-run farms as a valuable part of community and commerce.

Resources, including the USDA Web site, offer directories to CSA farms (see Resources). Ask neighbors, the produce manager at a natural foods store, the food editor of your local paper, and vendors at the farmers market for recommendations.

There are several criteria to consider when choosing a CSA membership for your family. The more information you gather, the more likely you are to feel satisfied and excited about your CSA membership. Consider the following:

Size of Farm CSAs vary in size, from farms such as Equinox CSA in Lincoln, Nebraska, with thirty-plus shareholders, to Be Wise Ranch, a 400-acre organic farm in San Diego with more than eight hundred CSA shareholders. A larger CSA farm may have more delivery or pickup locations and more membership options, but you'll have less direct contact with the farm, and the experience may be less personal.

Farming Practices What are the farm's growing methods? CSAs vary in farming practices. While many are certified organic, some practice biodynamic farming or use other methods.

Portrait of a CSA: Hedgerow Farm

Hedgerow Farm is a 20-acre farm in Boulder, Colorado, that has been certified organic since 1987 and managed biodynamically by farmer Jim Barausky since 1996.[6] "The farm has a long history of ownership and is now fully owned by Naropa University," says Hedgerow spokesperson Cheryl Mulholland. "Jim and I have built up the project from scratch. The previous owners had a falling out and the project was abandoned for several years until we came on the scene. Today our CSA has over ninety members, and we have a booming gourmet restaurant business. We are also very active in city and county politics in relationship to the GMO issues. We also give classes and seminars and public events here."

"In addition to the personal benefits of joining a CSA, community-supported agriculture has far-reaching social and political implications," Hedgerow's brochure says. "A CSA . . . is a direct relationship between consumer and the farmers of a community. Joining a CSA is a healthy social, political, and personal choice. It is an innovative approach to sustainability that connects people to the place they live, and to the people in their community, and allows them to share the responsibility for stewardship of the land and its resources. It is the ultimate in community action."

Hedgerow offers twenty-two-week memberships in two sizes, with an optional flower share. Early season crops include chives, mints, spinach, radishes, sprouts, lettuce, kale, turnips, scallions, and more. Summer brings basil, beets, carrots, cilantro, tomatoes, beans, broccoli, cauliflower, seasonal flowers, and more. And autumn harvests include winter squashes, root vegetables, and more of the cool-weather greens and salads. Members receive a weekly newsletter with recipes, upcoming events, and classes. Two pickup sites are available—a farmers market and on-farm—where "members choose, weigh, and package their own vegetables from bulk crates of freshly-harvested produce."

Hedgerow offers a volunteer program, classes, and community events. There are classes for children and adults, including organic gardening, bee-keeping, medicinal and cosmetic herbal products, and crafts. In conjunction with Naropa University, the farm offers an accredited ten-week course in sustainable agriculture. And farm celebrations are held for Earth Day, midsummer, and harvest.

In 2000, Hedgerow memberships cost $300 for a basic share and $550 for a family share. Shares that aren't picked up are donated to people in need.

"Through the food they receive in their weekly harvest, members gain a relationship to the living rhythms of the seasons," says Hedgerow's brochure. "And they learn about new foods such as Italian rapini or kohlrabi, which grow well in our climate. The weekly harvest results in a varied diet that reflects the healthful practice of eating freshly-harvested seasonal foods, a long-standing tradition among indigenous cultures and even our own culture before agribusiness created a global food economy."

Hedgerow's affiliation with Naropa University, a private university in Boulder, may lend it more educational focus than many farms, though the ideas and programs could work anywhere.

Crops Consider both the variety and type of crops. Do you want just seasonal basics or everything from herbs to flowers as well as foods? Some farms offer unusual crops, such as heirloom vegetables; these can be absolutely wonderful for cooks and foodies, but if your family hates to try new foods, you might be frustrated.

Delivery/Pickup Options A CSA membership is only as good as your ability to get the food in a timely and reasonably convenient way. Be sure that pickup locations and schedules work for you.

Cost Costs vary for a season of membership. Many farms offer levels of membership, so you can start small if you like. Consider splitting a membership with friends or neighbors if your family is small.

Participation Some farms will let you pick your own share or otherwise participate in farming activities. It can be a fantastic way to meet other members, involve kids, and get out of a daily life where you're surrounded by concrete. Evaluate your interest, time, and ability to participate if this is an option.

Experience CSAs that have been operating for many years usually have their systems worked out. A newer CSA may still have some growing pains, but also might let you help in its development. Again, it's a matter of interest and time.

Extras Ask about extras like newsletters, recipes, and farm events like pumpkin picking before Halloween and farm tours.

SUMMARY

- Organic foods are available today not just in natural foods stores but in supermarkets, co-op stores, even "big box" discount stores such as Costco and Wal-Mart. Each shopping choice has different strengths for the organic shopper. While natural foods stores have the greatest selection, others may have lower prices on some commodities or offer the convenience of general merchandise as well as organic choices.
- Availability of organic foods is increasing as more consumers become aware of the benefits of organic and ask for the organic choice.
- Farmers markets and community-supported agriculture allow consumers to buy directly from farmers, a practice with benefits from food freshness to better integrating agriculture into our communities.

CHAPTER ELEVEN

Is Organic Food More Nutritious?

The question of whether organic food is more nutritious than food grown with agricultural chemicals comes up all the time. It's a different question than whether pesticides are bad for you. Even if you accept that pesticide residues in food put many of us, especially children, at risk and that pesticides in the environment are a public health danger, it still begs the question of nutritional content. Does a carrot grown in organic soil have more beta-carotene than one grown in a chemical soup?

Intuitively, it makes a lot of sense that organically grown food is more nutritious, bite for bite, than conventionally grown food, and it's what a lot of people believe to be true. Rich, fertile soil packed with natural nutrients—how could it not yield a fruit, vegetable, or grain also richer in nutrients than those grown on a factory farm? And organic food is likely to be fresher, since no synthetic preservatives are used; conventionally grown food is more likely to be warehoused, transported long distances, or have its ripening artificially slowed.

But that illustrates an important point. There are so many factors beyond just the use or absence of chemicals that affect nutritional value and our ability to measure it accurately. From varietal differences to freshness, storage, transportation, and growing regions and microclimates, the multiplicity of variables makes straightforward scientific comparison of food groups challenging. Conventional foods are sometimes fortified with synthetic vitamins, often after having had the nutritious parts of the plant removed, leaving foods that have nutritional value but are heavily processed. Because of the inherent difficulties in obtaining measurements of nutritional value and drawing broad conclusions from them, reliable data are scarce.[1]

In other words, we just don't know, in a quantifiable, scientifically accurate way, if organic food is more nutritious, though consumer interest may drive scientists to create better research models in time. I like to argue that organic food is much more wholesome, and I'll get to that. But as for the simple, direct question of whether organic food is more nutritious, the answer is: It hasn't been proved.

A second answer is: It's the wrong question. Organic is not a health claim. It's a claim about a food production system and all that that implies for our communities and our world. Even if that bite-for-bite comparison leaves organic and conventionally grown food in a dead heat on nutritional value, organic food remains the best choice for environmental reasons, for the existence of small and family farmers, for our connection to those farmers and the work they do, and for protection of our right, as consumers, to know how our food is produced from field to table.

Interestingly, recently published research suggests that the nutritional content of conventionally grown food is declining. *Organic View,* the newsletter of the Organic Consumers Association of Little Marais, Minnesota, cites two such studies. First, the Kushi Institute, a macrobiotic education center in Becket, Massachusetts, examined USDA nutrient data over a twenty-two-year span ending in 1997. Average levels of calcium, iron, vitamin A, and vitamin C had all declined significantly in twelve fresh vegetables, with iron content dropping 37 percent. Another study found declines in calcium, iron, and potassium in vegetables grown in Britain during a fifty-year period (1930–1980).

The reasons for these significant declines are not fully clear, but chemical agriculture is one possible culprit. Factory farming techniques of heavy chemical fertilizer and pesticide use and monocropping deplete nutrients in the soil over time. Organic food, on the other hand, makes soil fertility and health a priority.

WHOLESOME FOOD

Because nutritional value is related to soil quality, organic food may very well be more nutritious than conventionally grown food. It's likely to be free of chemical residues, which can be systemic as well as on the surface of our foods and thus impossible to rinse off. So although organic is not a health claim, there are good reasons to think it may mean better health in the long run. But there are also less tangible yet very real ways that our well-being benefits from making the organic choice.

When we opt for organically grown food over conventionally grown food, we have to think about food in a way that's become very rare. We have to think about where our food comes from. It's become legend in the organic community that modern American children, when asked where food comes from, reply that it comes from the store. We've lost any awareness that food comes from a farm—that milk comes from a cow fed on grain, that peas come from pea pods on plants grown in soil—and that human beings cultivate our crops.

These connections may seem painfully obvious when we look at it this way, but the truth is that for most of us they're long forgotten, if we ever made them at all. It doesn't even matter if we're only a generation or two away from ancestors who farmed for a living and who may have given up a great deal for the opportunity to farm.

Food eaten with an understanding of its source is more wholesome food. Our relationship to food has a different quality when the farm it came from has a familiar name. Even if the farm isn't familiar or the food is processed, choosing the organic option often means supporting a small or family farm. Conventional farming is called factory farming for a reason: The human connection is absent, as machines and computers and chemicals churn out food with a sameness that cheats us of nature's vast diversity and richness and the deep nourishment we can find there.

High levels of efficiency in food production come from cultivating sameness, and sometimes that can be desirable. Convenience is of value, too, and few of us want to give up entirely the processed, frozen, and fast foods that can make our lives easier. But too much sameness and too much processing rob us of an abundance of flavor and variety. Wholesomeness comes in part from the richness that is available to us when food is grown with a commitment to biological diversity, flavor, and natural—not artificially enhanced—nutrition, as is organic food.

Joan Dye Gussow, Ed.D., a professor emeritus of nutrition and education at Teachers College of Columbia University and a former consumer representative to the National Organic Standards Board, wrote a response to the question "Is organic food more nutritious?" for *Eating Well* magazine in 1997. After reviewing the little research that had thus far been done on nutritional comparisons for organic food and noting its flaws, she concluded that, much as we may wish it otherwise, no reliable data existed at that time to suggest that organic is more nutritious:

> There's plenty of anecdotal evidence, but little hard proof that organically grown produce is reliably more nutritious. But being healthful is different than being more nutritious. After poring over the cumulative evidence from seventy years' worth of studies, the sum total strongly suggests that food grown according to organic principles is likely to have a variety of qualities that should, over the long term, make it more healthful. For example, organic foods usually have few, if any, chemical residues, and lower levels of nitrate nitrogen. These facts in and of themselves, while not a statement about nutritional values, make organic foods healthier. And even if the organic growing *process* doesn't make food more nutritious, many organic farmers use older, more nutritious cultivars. Additionally, because organic farmers protect the soil and avoid toxic chemicals, their practices have less of a deleterious impact on the environment—making them, one could say, more *wholesome*.[2]

Greater nutritional value in the entire category of organic foods may not be provable. But all things being equal, that organic carrot will more likely have been grown in conditions that nourish both soil and humans without potential harm, and that may reveal to us, if we are willing, a joyous connection to the earth and to those who grow our food.

SUMMARY

- Organic food has not been proved more nutritious than conventionally grown food.
- Organic is not a health claim, but a claim about a system of food production.

- Reasons to support organic food are valid independent of nutritional comparisons between organic and other food.
- Organic farming brings a lot to the table. Organic food offers us wholesome food that can reconnect us to the source of our nourishment.

CHAPTER TWELVE

Genetically Modified Foods and the Organic Alternative

If you shop at a conventional grocery store, it's possible that a great deal of the food available to you there has genetically modified (GM) ingredients.[1] These foods carry no labels to indicate that they've been produced with genetic modification, also called genetic engineering, genetic alteration, agricultural biotechnology, or transgenic technology. Corn-based and soy-based ingredients are the most common GM foods, in everything from carbonated sodas to corn chips to infant formula. What does this mean for you and your family? Should it worry you, and do you have alternatives?

Under the USDA's national organic standards, finalized in late 2000, and under private and state organic certification guidelines predating implementation of the national standards, *"certified organic" is the only regulated labeling system that specifically prohibits food from being grown or produced using genetic modification.*[2] To understand the great value of this guarantee provided by the organic label, you must first understand what genetic modification is and why many environmentalists, farmers, and nutritionists believe we simply do not have enough knowledge about long-term consequences to embrace this technology without limits—or without, at the very least, the clear and complete labeling of foods and ingredients produced with it.

No one knows for certain right now if agricultural biotechnology can be used without harming humans or the environment in either the short or long term. The harsh lessons we've learned from decades of using inadequately tested pesticides should tell us to proceed with utmost caution. Furthermore, the advantages of unlabeled genetically modified foods are skewed heavily toward multinational chemical corporations, rather than farmers or eaters. This goes against the principles of a food system in which consumers have full knowledge and full participation. The organic choice becomes even more important in this scheme, with transgenic technologies already in widespread use and on the shelves of our grocery stores.

WHAT IS GENETIC MODIFICATION?

Genetic modification is a process by which genetic material from one species—segments of DNA with particular, predetermined traits—is inserted into the DNA of another species. Foreign genetic material can be transferred from bacteria into plants, from animals into plants, and from other species into animals. This differs from traditional plant breeding, which primarily cultivates desirable traits within species but doesn't transfer genetic material across vastly different species.[3]

Primarily, transgenic technology has been used to create plants that emit their own pesticides, ostensibly limiting the chemicals that must be applied in the environment, or that are designed to withstand powerful chemical applications so that herbicides can be used with impunity and (theoretically) affect only undesirable plants. Monsanto's Roundup Ready technology is probably the best known of this latter use of genetic modification. Plants such as soybeans are engineered to resist Roundup, Monsanto's brand of the herbicide glyphosate, allowing farmers to use even more Roundup without worrying about killing crops.

In some cases, foreign genes are used to slow ripening of fruits and vegetables or to increase traits desirable to growers. Tomatoes and strawberries, for example, have been engineered with fish genes to keep them viable at colder temperatures.

HOW WIDESPREAD IS GENETIC MODIFICATION?

A Consumers Union study estimated that genetically engineered crops in 1999 covered one-fourth of America's farmland, or 90 million acres. In crop percentages, that included more than 35 percent of corn, more than half of all soybeans, and close to half of all cotton.[4]

In the United States today, genetically engineered crops include canola, chicory, corn, cotton, flax, papaya, potatoes, soybeans, squash, sugar beets, and tomatoes. The foreign genetic material for most of these crops is DNA from bacteria.[5]

Many foods contain ingredients that are derivatives of these plants, such as corn oil. In fact, if you look carefully at labels, you'll find these crops in some form in countless processed foods (as well as in the form of fresh produce). Some of these products, such as soy, are also used in dietary supplements and body care products.

A few companies have taken steps to limit genetically modified ingredients. McDonald's, in a widely publicized move, asked its potato growers to stop using GM seed, though this doesn't mean that other ingredients the company buys are not engineered. Others, like Guiltless Gourmet, a Texas-based maker of baked corn chips, have not only renounced GM crops but have gone all the way to earning organic certification for their products. Two major natural foods chains, Wild Oats of Boulder, Colorado, and Whole Foods Market of Austin, Texas, have said that they will remove genetically modified ingredients from their storebrand products. This does not mean, of course, that other foods in the store are not produced with genetic modification (unless those foods are certified organic).

But many mainstream manufacturers continue to use GM ingredients, at least in the United States, where consumer resistance hasn't risen to the levels seen in Europe and Japan. According to the Organic Consumers Association, based in Little Marais, Minnesota (www.purefood.org), these include Safeway, Coca-Cola, Nabisco, Quaker Oats, Starbucks, General Mills, Kraft, Healthy Choice, and more. If you have concerns about any product you buy, contact the company's consumer service department via the Web or telephone and insist on disclosure of genetically modified ingredients. This includes products labeled "natural." There are no regulations limiting the use of the "natural" label; though some companies specify that "natural" means no preservatives, which is, as we have seen, very different from the absence of GM ingredients.

WHO REALLY BENEFITS?

What are the advantages of transgenic technology, and who reaps the rewards? Chemical manufacturers such as Monsanto, Novartis, and DuPont have invested many millions of dollars in its development and recently announced a joint public relations campaign, for which they'll pay $50 million or more, to convince Americans of the value of genetically engineered foods. These companies are the primary beneficiaries of genetic engineering—not farmers, not consumers, and not, unfortunately, developing countries with starving and undernourished populations, as proponents of agricultural biotechnology would have you believe.[6,7]

Farmers who've been convinced to use this technology must buy seeds that have been deliberately made sterile, so they can't save seeds for replanting, which would help them save money each year. And the farmers are then locked into buying seeds and chemicals from the same company; essentially, they lose control of their crops, with farm inputs and outputs determined by outsiders who profit at both ends.

Chemical manufacturers, who now use the euphemism "life science companies," delivered genetically modified foods in mass quantity to grocery shelves without asking consumers if that's what they want, and without labels. As consumers began to question the wisdom and safety of this technology, the same companies suggested that consumers were simply too ignorant to understand the value of genetic modification and too stupid not to be unnecessarily frightened by complete labels. These same chemical companies are now saying that if consumers insist on foods produced without genetic engineering, we'll all have to pay more for it because it will cost money to segregate genetically modified harvests from non-GM crops.

I believe that consumers should be outraged by this manipulation of the food supply and of our wallets. The trail of benefits, which are primarily financial despite these companies' attempts at spin control that suggests otherwise, leads right back to the already deep pockets of these multinational corporations. They need new profit centers as reevaluation of pesticide risk leads the government to restrict the production and use of the chemicals that have brought these companies such enormous profits in the past.

Consumers don't benefit much from genetically modified foods, unless your main concern is foods with longer shelf life, self-generating pesticides and herbicides, or other traits that have little to do with quality or flavor but that benefit large-scale factory farming, still based on a pesticide model rather than one of healthy soil and natural resistance, and inexpensive warehousing of foods—though not necessarily inexpensive to you.

There are several ways to let these companies know that you're more interested in the quality of the food supply than in their multimillion-dollar profits and executive bonuses. Let your grocery store, your legislative representatives, and the food manufacturers know in no uncertain terms that you want genetically modified foods to be labeled clearly and that you will make the choice to buy non-GM alternatives whenever and wherever you can. And then make good on that threat by buying organic foods.

CONSUMER REACTION

Consumers in Europe, Japan, and certain other countries have waged a fierce battle against genetically modified foods. They've been so outspoken in their rejection of these foods that companies can no longer plant genetically engineered crops with impunity, few grocery stores will sell them, and even some of our world leaders, including England's Prince Charles, have advocated against them.

In this country, however, fewer consumers feel knowledgeable about the process of genetic engineering or have any real sense of the potential consequences or actual benefits. The superficial spin of the chemical companies—that GM foods are good for the environment because they make their own pesticides or that this technology is necessary to "feed the world"—belies their own unwillingness to label these foods and let consumers make the choice or to do adequate safety testing to assess the long-term risks.

American opposition to genetically engineered foods is growing, however. Food manufacturers have acknowledged that they're in the business of giving consumers what they want and will not continue to pursue genetically modified ingredients if resistance is strong enough. Others have said they feel the "timing" is wrong and that consumers must be "educated" about what's good for them before transgenic technology can really take its full (unlabeled) place in the market. At the same time, environmentalists, growers, and others have the opportunity to educate consumers about the other perspective—that genetically modified foods take us one step further away from a wholesome, sustainable agriculture and food industry.

WHAT ARE THE POTENTIAL
ENVIRONMENTAL CONSEQUENCES?

Genetically engineered plants create a kind of environmental infiltration that cannot be contained once released. Widespread adoption of this technology has not been proved environmentally safe. Everything that pesticides have taught us indicates that introducing transgenic plants on a large scale will have consequences for everything else in the ecosphere. Until we know what those consequences are and how they will be controlled, if necessary, we are taking a dramatic and dangerous gamble.[8]

Although companies invested in transgenic technology insist that its use will result in less pesticide use, so far that has not always been the case. In some cases, pesticide use has even increased. Pests are likely to become resistant to pesticide-producing plants, just as they've become resistant to applied chemicals. And plants that have been genetically engineered to withstand weedkiller may encourage farmers to use more weedkiller.[9]

Genetically engineered plants may generate ecological changes that cannot be controlled. We know from experience with applied agricultural chemicals that insects and plants can develop resistance to chemical herbicides and pesticides fairly quickly. The specter of a "superweed" that cannot be controlled without creating new chemicals is very possible.

The principle of interdependence, a key element in organic agriculture, tells us that we cannot make radical changes to one part of an ecosystem without affecting the other parts. In the case of transgenic crops, those unpredictable changes may adversely affect populations of birds, butterflies, and bees, to name just a few trends that have already been observed by scientists.

Another frightening potential development of genetically modified crops is a progressive weakening of certain natural pesticides widely used by organic farmers. Inserting pest-killing genes into large acreages of common plant crops may also aggressively accelerate the rate at which insects can develop resistance to these substances. Some of these are important natural resorts for organic farmers and can mean the difference between saving a crop and losing it. Once insect populations develop resistance, organic farmers are deprived of an important alternative.[10]

Furthermore, as we've seen, transgenic plants will contaminate organic crops to some degree through background dispersion in the environment. The wholesale introduction of this technology without explicit consumer consent means it is imposed on all of us to some degree. It's another form of pollution that requires our determined opposition.

WHAT ARE THE POTENTIAL HEALTH CONSEQUENCES?

While no one has proved these foods safe in the long term, there is also no proof right now that they're not. Right now we don't know. One concern with the transplant of foreign genes and the lack of labeling is allergenicity, both from known allergens and possible new allergens that might be generated as an unexpected consequence of foreign gene insertion.

But so far, there isn't conclusive evidence of health consequences directly traceable to genetically modified ingredients in food. Does this justify giving a green light and no speed limit to this technology? Again, "not proved dangerous" is not the same as "proved safe." And time after time, our live experiment with pesticides has shown that something invisible and seemingly benign in the short term can have unalterable, undesirable, and unforeseen consequences in the long term, sometimes in ways that only reveal themselves across several generations.

There's another very real consequence of grocery shelves and dinner plates full of genetically engineered food and the system of multinational chemical corporations that has created and promoted this technology. It takes us exponentially further away from a wholesome and healthy relationship with food—from our understanding of where food comes from and how it's produced. It also further removes our ability to know and trace how companies have handled our food supply from start to finish. And a lack of labeling limits accountability on the part of the very companies that wish to profit so enormously from this technology.

WHY NO LABELS?

In the United States, the majority of consumers say that labels on genetically engineered foods make sense.[11] The food industry lobbies hard against such labeling, saying it will "needlessly scare" consumers. It's just one more example of an arrogant food industry insisting that consumers shouldn't make informed decisions—that whatever fears consumers have are automatically groundless and whatever control they hope to exert over their own food intake is undeserved.

Consumers, of course, are far more interested in health and safety than in ignoring misgivings so that food companies and multinational chemical companies will profit. And labeling also allows all of us to track accountability. If negative health or environmental consequences do result from this unasked-for technology, labeling will make it much easier to trace those responsible for unleashing it without adequate testing or evaluation. And a lack of labeling, of course, will make it that much harder to assess responsibility.

What exactly are food manufacturers afraid of? Undoubtedly, their worst nightmare is a straightforward label on foods engineered with transgenic technology. Reality would hit home if those bright red strawberries carried a label that read "Contains genetic material from fish," or if sweet corn were labeled "Contains foreign genetic material from bacteria that kills pests."

In a strange way, these labels might finally communicate to consumers that pesticides, whether externally applied or internally administered through genetic engineering, are toxic chemicals that, for the most part, haven't been adequately evaluated for use in foods. If true and complete labels delineating everything used to produce the foods we buy make us uncomfortable, maybe more of us will stop assuming that these chemicals and technologies are universally "safe" and without environmental consequences. And then we might see the dream of many organic farmers come true—a world where organically produced food requires no labels and no justification while conventional, chemically produced foods must be labeled and highly regulated in their entirety.

WHAT ABOUT FEEDING THE WORLD?

Proponents of genetic modification in agriculture often claim that this technology is necessary to feed the world, that developing countries with food shortages and population increases make it necessary to increase yields on farmland. But their arguments ring false. It has been shown that food shortages are due to problems of distribution rather than of the world not making enough food.[12] And studies at the Rodale Institute are building a body of information that backs up organic farming as equivalent in production yields, or nearly equivalent, to conventional farming.[13] This means that organic production methods have as much potential to feed the world as others, but with far less risk and degradation to the environment.

Companies also argue that genetically engineered "golden rice"—rice with a gene inserted to produce higher levels of vitamin A—is the answer to vitamin deficiencies in the Third World. Again, they make the claim without discussing the consequences of this technology, strategies for distribution, and alternative methods of getting vitamin A to children in need. Some proponents have appropriated a tragic problem to appear as if their solution were the only one and that to oppose unlabeled transgenic technologies in the food supply is to oppose feeding children. While I don't doubt the sincerity of scientists who would like to address the tragedy of malnutrition, I am admittedly cynical about the motivations of some who I believe are using this problem to justify widespread, untested, unlabeled genetic modification of foods throughout the developed world.

If vitamin A in the Third World is a concern of yours—and it is indeed a serious problem—support one of the organizations offering immediate help to these children instead of investing millions in an unproved and potentially dangerous technology that may hurt communities.[14] Until we know more about the real consequences of widespread transgenic technologies, we can use immediate avenues of distribution to get vitamins to those in need.

VOICE YOUR CONCERNS

The issue of transgenic technology in the food supply should be of vital concern to consumers. Opposition to the way this technology is currently being insinuated into the food supply doesn't have to mean that you are antiscience, antitechnology, or against, for example, carefully designed and transparently conducted research using genetic engineering that may have true social benefits. Science and humanitarian and environmental concerns are not inherently in opposition to each other, though some chemical companies and their advocates imply as much to discredit those who are concerned about genetically engineered foods.

But to be confident in expressing your opposition when you feel it's appropriate, you have to be informed. It's not an especially fun or sexy topic for most of us to examine. It would be much easier to just stay in denial—to assume that the government is always right, always protecting us, and always acting in our best interests rather than in the interests of large, multibillion-dollar corporations.

So learn what you can and voice your concerns. First of all, vote with your dollars: Buy organically grown foods. Then support companies that reject genetically modified ingredients in food and that do so throughout the supply chain and in a way that's accountable. Again, let your legislative representatives know that you expect them to support the labeling of foods with genetically engineered ingredients—not euphemistic labeling designed to mollify or confuse consumers, but complete and straightforward labeling. Let your grocery store manager know the same, or write to the store's corporate executives.

Consumers, by and large, want the same things. They want safe, nutritious, high-quality food, and they don't want to be snowed by dubious claims. In England, even the company cafeteria in Monsanto's U.K. offices won't serve genetically engineered foods, because the majority of the employees were so uncomfortable with the idea. Do they know something we don't? Or do they, like many others, just want much better assurances and proofs of safety before giving our wholesale approval to this technology? Either way, we all should know enough by now about careless use of powerful methods to want a little more knowledge and control over our food supply than current genetic engineering practices allow.

SUMMARY

- Genetically modified organisms, where foreign genes are spliced into organisms that would not naturally be able to produce them, have not been proved safe for health or the environment and have serious potential risks for both.
- Transgenic ingredients nonetheless are being used in a great deal of America's food supply, though this food is not labeled and the conventional food industry is fighting against labeling.
- Chemical and agribusiness companies are the ones likely to profit from this technology, rather than farmers, consumers, or developing countries, in spite of public relations claims.
- Organic agriculture does not use genetically modified seeds, plants, or ingredients.

CHAPTER THIRTEEN

Organic on a Budget

As I was writing this chapter, I went to my local conventional grocery store—which carries a pretty good selection of organic and natural foods—and stood in the produce section near a woman desperately seeking a ripe avocado. "I need one for dinner tonight," she said. "These are all hard as a rock."

I gestured back toward the organic foods section. "There's a whole table of ripe ones back there," I said. "I know," the woman said. "They're organic, and they're $2.49 each." Though the organic fruit was just what she needed, that choice was clearly out of the question for her.

I thought about pointing out that at least with an organic avocado she could plant the seed and expect to have a beautiful plant, an unlikely event with chemically treated fruit. Instead, I silently tried to honor her concerns and realized anew that for many consumers, the value of organics is a little mysterious.

I don't know what this woman's economic situation was, and whether spending an additional 50 cents on an avocado would have really been a hardship for her. I do know that every purchase we make involves a complex combination of factors: perceived worth, perceived quality, our own economic situation, our emotions about money and how we spend it, and, for many shoppers, intangible values such as environmental and health benefits.

But cost is also relative to what we're used to paying and what we think something should cost. The woman in the grocery store couldn't see the difference between those two avocados, except that one cost more. Naturally, I think her best choice would have been to buy the organic avocado for all the right reasons, or at least to buy it wishing it cost less but knowing it would be a vote with her dollar for a better food system.

For me, that organic avocado made good sense. For one thing, a bargain is only a bargain if it fills your needs. My fellow shopper needed a ripe avocado that night; an unripe one, even if less expensive, would be useless to her. More important, that organic avocado would feed a whole set of values that matter to me. I suspect those values would matter to her, too, if she had more information about the benefits of organic foods and the reasons why they cost more and why conventional foods cost less, which is not as straightforward as many of us think.

My own purchases that day were a mix of organic and conventional choices; even the most committed among us balance many factors as we buy. But many shoppers think it has to be all or nothing; they feel like hypocrites if they buy a box of Oreo cookies along with organic carrots and cereal. You can disregard that notion right now. Every organic choice is meaningful, and you don't have to subscribe to anybody else's rules. Buying organic says something about your values, but it doesn't define who you are, who you vote for, or what you drive. It's likely that as you understand the values and benefits of organic agriculture, values of environmentalism, health, and consumers' rights will also affect other decisions you make, but the choices are all yours. Be informed, make the best choices you can make, and start small, with just a few organic foods, if that's what you're comfortable with.

There are ways to cut costs even when buying organic, and there are guidelines for making good choices when you can't buy everything organic. If you have children six years of age or younger, I'd make organic foods a priority for them, especially baby food, fruits and vegetables, and fruit-based products such as juice (and be sure juices for this age-group are pasteurized). From there, certain foods are, as a whole, more contaminated than others. Personally, I've lost my taste for strawberries unless I know they're organic.

Truthfully, if that organic avocado on my shopping trip had been twice the price of the conventionally grown one, I might have turned it down, too, looking instead for a dinner recipe with more seasonal or less costly items, where the organic choice would have been possible without going far beyond my own economic comfort level. We all have a price threshold. But educated consumers can sometimes make an intelligent choice to spend more, within reason, in support of a food system that respects our right to know what we're eating.

WHY DO ORGANIC FOODS COST MORE?

Why do organic foods cost more? In part, because the cost of conventionally grown food is artificially low and does not reflect the true cost of bringing food to market—and certainly does not reflect the cost of righting the environmental ills of agribusiness as usual.[1] Organic Trade Association (OTA) literature explains that "there is mounting evidence that if all the indirect costs of conventional food production (cleanup of polluted water, replacement of eroded soils, costs of health care for farmers and their workers, etc.) were factored into the price of food, organic foods would cost the same, or more likely, be cheaper."[2]

Other reasons that organic food costs more, according to OTA, include more labor- and management-intensive systems; smaller operations without the economies of scale of conventionally grown foods; costs of organic compliance; and an absence of farm subsidization programs that offset the costs of conventional farming (but which we do pay for in taxes and which give little support to small farms). And of course, basic rules of supply and demand apply. Right now there is more demand for organic food than consistent supply, so these foods can command higher prices.

Fortunately, farmers can command higher prices as well, though of course the profit margin for growers varies with different sources. If you're buying at the farmers market, through a community-supported agriculture program, or through a co-op, the farmer is likely to see a greater return than if you're buying from a large grocer.

At the checkout stand, however, all these arguments may be meaningful but overridden by immediate economic concerns. Right now, supporters of organic and sustainable foods and products are pioneering changes in the marketplace—with some remarkable results. Yet, in a sense, we pay a penalty for that role, since our taxes continue to pay the costs of conventional agriculture, including environmental cleanup costs, even as we choose to spend more on food to support organics. While many of us feel that it's a penalty worth paying to bring change to the system, each of us must also balance this cause with our other needs and our budgets.[3]

On a personal level, then, we must arrive at solutions that put the most organic food on our table for the money we spend. This is the only way to keep organic food from becoming a fetish of the affluent rather than a joyful, all-inclusive restoration of healthful, sustainable eating.

Economists say that the costs of conventional agriculture are largely *externalized*—that is, they do not appear to have a direct link to the cost of making the product. Yet they must be considered as future costs to us all, especially our children. Some scientists estimate the cost of pesticide-related environmental and health costs in the billions of dollars.

At present, organically grown food in the market comes closer to re-flecting its true costs to society. Its costs are internalized, or built into the price you pay—more up front, but without the repair costs later on. This is why, by and large, organic growers cannot reduce their costs to compete with factory farms whose lower prices represent an ominous efficiency.

KEEPING COSTS DOWN

Are there ways to cut the price of organic meals? There are indeed. Con-sider these suggestions, grounded in the knowledge that prices do come down and the benefits of supporting organics will accrue:

- When possible, explore the options of farmers markets and community-supported agriculture (CSA) programs. With these avenues, you're buying directly from the farmer, and your dollars are truly supporting organic agriculture in the most immediate way.
- When buying fresh organic foods, choose those in season and, when possible, grown locally. Not only does it conserve energy lost in transportation and storage, but the price is likely to be lower and the food just-picked.
- Organic meals don't have to be fancy, even if some people equate "gourmet" with organic. Choose organic in the humble but healthy

staples that many natural foods stores sell in bulk (further reducing both packaging and price): rice, pasta, grains, beans, flours, cereals.

- Some of the most flavorful, nutritious, and colorful vegetables are also relatively inexpensive, like winter greens, the many varieties of squash that fill the market in autumn, and root vegetables.
- As organic and natural foods do become more widely available, price competition is heating up. Gaining popularity, too, are all the traditional methods of attracting customers: coupons, newspaper ads with sales, and special promotions. Take advantage!
- Natural foods stores often create colorful, informative in-store flyers and newsletters that highlight special bargains. Take some time to review these often.
- Try a little kitchen gardening. Just a few herbs in containers can add life to budget-minded food and save you money too.
- Involve your family. Talk with them about the cost of organic foods and where you might all agree to help in reducing some other costs to help support organics. Or make it a family project to research how foods are grown (some are more pesticide intensive than others) and choose specific foods that you'll always buy organic.
- Many stores give you a small refund when you bring your own bags. Invest in a few canvas bags and never agonize over the environmental costs of plastic versus paper again.[4] Then take those nickels you get for using your own bags and justify a few more organic purchases.
- If you must limit your organic purchases, the items your children eat should be organic when possible, now that we know that pesticides can have a proportionately greater harmful effect on children.
- Keep in mind that even in conventional markets, a wholesome, nutritious diet of fresh foods will cost more than a diet of processed junk foods, but will offer much more in real health value.
- Likewise, shopping for the best bargains, clipping coupons, and cooking at home all take more time than their costlier, though convenient, alternatives. In other words, sometimes it's just that healthy foods cost more, and saving money takes time.

- Finally, let your government representatives know that you want your taxpayer dollars used for organic farming research and support, that you want organics in school lunch programs, and that you want the environmental and health costs of dangerous pesticides to be paid by the businesses that profit from their sale and use.

ADDING ORGANIC FOODS TO YOUR KITCHEN

If buying organic is new for you, it's easy to start almost anywhere. But make it easy on yourself by buying familiar foods that you and your family already like. Start with salad foods in season and choose an organic olive oil or dressing, or try organic corn chips and salsa.

Organic popcorn is an easy switch to make. Organic milk is important for children, widely available, and can even be found in chocolate flavor. In fact, organic chocolate bars are easy to love too. If your kids want "real" toasted oats cereals or chocolate-covered candies, compromise there with conventional foods. But make the strawberries and bananas on the cereal organic, by all means.

FOOD SAFETY REMINDER

Remember that food safety is everyone's concern. Whether organic or conventional, foods can contain pathogens. Use judicious food safety practices and take special care for children, the elderly, and anyone with a compromised immune system:

- Wash produce thoroughly.
- Be sure milk and children's juices are pasteurized.
- Cook meats to proper temperatures.
- Don't let raw meat and poultry juices contact other foods.
- Keep foods refrigerated or frozen when called for.[5]

CAN PESTICIDES BE WASHED OFF?

If you're washing produce anyway, aren't you washing off the pesticides too? Yes, you are likely to wash off at least some of any external residues. Pesticides are also carried systemically into the body of the fruit and vegetable, however, and these cannot be washed off.[6]

What about those citric acid sprays? Again, if you're buying conventionally grown food, you may benefit from using these produce washes.

Either way, you're better off than if you do nothing. But remember that the benefits of organic agriculture go beyond the absence of pesticides. If you wash surface pesticides off, they've still been used and remain in our soil, air, and water.

SUMMARY

- Save money on organic foods by choosing seasonal foods and, whenever possible, foods grown close to home.
- Children under six are especially vulnerable to pesticide residues. When you have to choose, put the kids' food first for organic choices.
- Buy in bulk, choose a plant-based diet with less meat, and use all the tricks at hand—coupons, sales—to save money on organic foods.

CHAPTER FOURTEEN

Feed Your Children Well: Organic Foods in Your Children's Diet

One of the most important reasons for supporting organic agriculture is to protect the environment. But beyond that, there are many benefits to be reaped from the organic alternative to our food production system. Although the organic label tells you how the food is grown and is not a health claim per se—the label in and of itself doesn't mean organic foods are better for you—when it comes to children, organic foods may make an important contribution to setting the stage for lifelong health and optimal physical and mental development. An adult may not be vulnerable to bodily insult from eating foods with the level of pesticide residues often measured in sample foods. The same is not necessarily true for children, and many environmental health experts believe that the risks we currently accept are too high.

For this reason, this is one of the most important chapters of this book, and I hope you will read and consider it carefully, even though the information isn't pleasant. In this chapter, we focus not so much on the positive strengths of organics but on the very real potential dangers of pesticides. But the information available to us shouldn't make us feel helpless or hopeless. Postwar and baby boom generations lacked knowledge and choice about the dangers of children's exposure to pesticides and other chemicals, but today we know more and have alternatives. We can and must do better by today's children and future generations.

This book is dedicated to my nieces and nephews, because I see them as treasures both magnificent and vulnerable. My hope is that these beautiful young people will enjoy long lives with all the health and strength and opportunity they deserve. As parents, aunts, uncles, teachers, and guardians, it's something we all want for the children we love. But for that to happen, children must be protected from unsafe doses of powerful, often toxic chemicals.

GOOD ENOUGH FOR THE KIDS?

Some years ago, I worked for a chain of natural foods supermarkets as a public relations specialist. The company hired a manager with a background in the conventional supermarket industry. He moved his family out to Colorado from the Midwest and enthusiastically embraced the natural foods world, where he saw opportunity and growth. He also did a lot of homework on organic agriculture and came to understand it pretty well and appreciate its innovations.

But he was going down the wrong track in one critical way. As we were talking one day, this manager told me how he and his wife were buying more and more organic produce, especially fruit. But, he told me, he and his wife didn't feed the organic foods they were buying to their kids. Because organic costs more, the adults were eating organic while feeding conventionally grown food to their children.

That family's decision was logical based on what they knew, but they were missing a big part of the picture. The children, in all likelihood, needed the benefits and protection of organic foods more than the adults did. In the last decade, a host of studies have shown that infants and children are far more at risk from pesticide exposure than are adults. Furthermore, the EPA's standards for testing tolerances for pesticide exposure have never taken the risk profile of children into account, and only since 1996 has that agency been mandated to revise these risk assessments—a long, slow process so far.[1] Foods at the top of the most-contaminated list, including certain fruits and fruit juices, typically make up a much larger percentage of children's diets than adult diets, in terms of both quantity of food and calories in relation to body weight.[2, 3, 4] In infants' diets, water is also very important, and a great deal of water is contaminated with pesticides.[5]

All of this is complicated by the fact that the effects of long-term pesticide overexposure in children may be chronic rather than acute. Children at risk won't necessarily act or look like someone who has been poisoned. Instead, they may have increased health problems indirectly linked to chemical pollutants, such as asthma, allergies, and childhood incidence of cancer. Some environmental health specialists are even studying whether behavior problems can be linked to chemical exposure from foods and the environment.[6]

There is increasing evidence that when children with early and chronic exposure grow up, risk of adult disease or insufficiencies, such as breast cancer and low sperm count, may be multiplied owing to exposure during key developmental periods and to a greater lifetime toxic burden.[7] "Better living through chemistry" may have a dark side of enormous magnitude in terms of public health and our children's future.

BABY LOVE

New parents will do almost anything to keep their baby's environment free from visible, smelly dirt and germs. But it may very well be the chemicals that can't be seen or even smelled (and may not cause any immediate symptoms of illness) that are the most harmful. These chemicals are in everything from diapers, paints, new carpets, cleaning products, pesticides used in the home to keep it bug-free, and pesticides, herbicides, chemical fertilizers, artificial preservatives, and dyes used in foods. From the moment today's children are born, their bodies are assaulted with chemicals, from gases emitted by new furniture and carpets in pristine nurseries to chemicals in disposable diapers that turn liquids into gels.

Over a lifetime, this chemical assault can make for a very heavy toxic burden on the body, though effects may not show up for many years or even until the next generation begins to mature. Some effects may be "sins of omission," where a child never reaches full potential in mental capacity, coordination, memory, or other cognitive performance measures because of the actions of chemicals on nervous system development in early childhood. And some effects may be chronic and debilitating, but with many possible contributing causes, as is the case of asthma and allergies in young children—diseases increasing at an astonishing rate, especially in economically disadvantaged neighborhoods, where toxins may be even more concentrated.

These frightening consequences of chemical exposure are, by and large, the result of completely legal chemicals deemed "safe" by the federal government when applied according to established standards. But "safe" does not mean harmless by any means. Pesticides, for example, are specifically formulated to kill living things, often by damaging the target's nervous system; in other words, they are designed to be neurotoxins. Many of the hundreds of pesticides authorized for use in this country have documented links to cancer, infertility, diseases of the brain and nervous system, and birth deformities. It's just that the EPA has determined that, up to a point, the benefits of these chemicals outweigh the risks. In the past, those risks have been determined with very little knowledge of long-term effects.

In recent years, we've learned more about the way children absorb and process these chemicals, and it's become apparent that all the ways that governments and manufacturers have measured safety tolerances for these chemicals are utterly inadequate when it comes to infants and children. In the last decade, groundbreaking research has shed new light on the amount of pesticides children are ingesting and what their impact may be. A 1993 report issued by the National Academy of Sciences called "Pesticides in the Diets of Infants and Children" demonstrated the need for serious examination of children's diets. The information we have today paints a grim picture: Babies born today, whether breast-fed or bottle-fed, may be at risk for detrimental effects from conventional, chemical-based agriculture from the moment they're born.

Breast-feeding, which we now know to have many positive advantages for infants, also has the unfortunate disadvantage of being at the top of the food chain. Some of the most dangerous and persistent chemicals in the environment become more and more concentrated as they move up the food chain. Stored in fatty tissue such as breast tissue, these chemicals make breast milk a carrier of intensified toxins. "While prenatal exposure seems to pose the greatest hazard, health specialists also worry about the chemicals passed on in breast milk because some sensitive developmental processes continue in the weeks immediately after birth," Theo Colborn writes in *Our Stolen Future*:

> During breast feeding, human infants are exposed to higher concentrations of these chemicals than at any subsequent time in their lives. In just six months of breast feeding, a baby in the United States and Europe gets the maximum recommended lifetime dose of dioxin, which rides through the food web like PCBs [polychlorinated biphenyls] and DDT [dichloro-diphenyl-trichloroethane]. The same breast feeding baby gets five times the allowable daily level of PCBs set by international health standards for a 150-pound adult.[8]

Formula-fed babies fare little better. A study released in 1999 by Environmental Working Group (EWG) showed that atrazine, one of the most widely used agricultural herbicides, contaminated tap water in almost eight hundred towns in the Midwest.[9] That same tap water is often used to dilute concentrated infant formula. Some tap water is so contaminated that infants get their lifetime limit of atrazine before they are four months old, EWG says. In June 2000, the EPA changed the classification of atrazine from "possible carcinogen" to "likely carcinogen." The EPA had *never before* looked thoroughly at the chemical's risk to children. When it did, it concluded that even short-term exposure to atrazine has the potential to affect the normal development of reproductive organs and capabilities.[10]

Atrazine is an agricultural chemical that the government told us was "safe" for many years. Tap water has always been analyzed by computing average annual levels of chemical residues, but where agricultural runoff is concerned, levels spike at certain times during the year. So short-term exposure has been a very real possibility even when official records would show a "safe" level in community water supplies.

And the population most threatened by these inadequate methods of calculating exposure levels are the youngest members of our communities. Water makes up a large part of the diets of infants as the dilutant for infant formula and fruit juices.

Ingredients of infant formula itself may also be of concern. Formula made with conventionally grown corn or soy are more likely than not to include transgenic, or genetically modified, ingredients. Monosodium glu-tamate, a neurotoxin, and allergenic ingredients also appear in analyses of infant formula. Even the plastic bottles used to feed infants may be sus-pect because of hormone-disrupting chemicals that warm liquids in the bottles can absorb.[11]

New or soon-to-be parents may well be wondering which option they should choose in this dance with chemical devils: breast-feeding or bottle-feeding. There are many factors to consider, including the mother's age (with age, breast tissue accumulates more toxins unless they are expressed through milk), where the mother lives and has lived (rural or urban areas), and what the choices are for formula made with organic ingredients and free of questionable ingredients. Inform yourself, talk with doctors, read the work of environmental health experts and pediatricians, and try to do it without making yourself crazy. As a forty-two-year-old woman, if I were to become pregnant, I would want to breast-feed, but would probably consult an environmental health specialist familiar with hormone-disrupting chemicals to review my history before I made the choice.[12]

Meanwhile, inform your elected representatives that you expect them to push the EPA to quickly complete the revised risk assessments mandated by the Food Quality Protection Act of 1996 and that you want public health to be of higher priority in their legislative activities than the interests of the chemical manufacturers. And vote with your dollars to support alternatives to a chemical-based food system whenever and however you can.

GROWING CHILDREN AT RISK

It's frightening to see that the real risks of pesticide exposure, via breast milk or bottle formula, appear before a child even begins to drink juice or eat solid food. And then the real fun begins. Those foods your kids love and that you want them to eat—strawberries, peaches, spinach—are some of the most contaminated foods.[13, 14] And children are affected more by eat-ing them. Fortunately, there are now more organically grown and pro-duced foods that reflect children's tastes. From cereals to milk, juice to macaroni and cheese, organic options are multiplying. Doing the right nutritional thing—getting your kids to eat lots of fresh fruits and vegetables—makes the right choice at the market even more important.

In brief, children may be at risk from pesticide exposure for both physical and dietary reasons. Physically, infants and children are undergoing rapid growth driven by organ development and cell reproduction. A child reaches half his or her adult height very early on—within the first few years of life. Periods of rapid development such as these may correlate to much greater susceptibility to the detrimental effects of many chemicals.[15] Rapid growth and development of immature organs and bodily systems also requires a body functioning at a much higher metabolic rate than that typical of fully developed adults. This means that the intake of calories to fuel growth is much higher in proportion to body weight than it is for adults. So, relative to size, young children are eating much more.

Children's diets also generally include higher proportions of fruits, fruit-based foods and liquids, and fresh vegetables.[16] The quality and purity—or lack thereof—of these foods therefore become of paramount importance. It also further illustrates the failure of our current system to analyze pesticide risk, since these dietary concentrations are not accounted for. Pesticide tolerances have been evaluated in terms of the chemicals' effects on full-size, mature adult males and the effects of single chemicals, although agricultural chemicals tend to be used in combination, and humans generally ingest several foods at a time, each of which may have different chemical residues.

Now, down to specifics. In 1995, Environmental Working Group commissioned a study of pesticides in three major baby food brands: Gerber, Heinz, and Beech-Nut. According to their report, titled "Pesticides in Baby Food:"

> Sixteen pesticides were detected in the eight baby food products tested, including three probable human carcinogens, five possible human carcinogens, eight neurotoxins, five pesticides that disrupt the normal functioning of the hormone system [endocrine disrupters], and five pesticides that are categorized as oral toxicity one, the most toxic designation . . . Iprodione (Rovral), classified by the EPA as a probable human carcinogen, was found

more often and at higher levels than any other pesticide detected, even though it was found only in peaches and plums.[17]

It's important to note that the pesticide residues were well below federal standards, so the companies were not negligent in terms of limits set by law. "But federal pesticide standards do not specifically incorporate any special protection for infants or young children," the report cautions. The good news is that those standards have been mandated for revision by the Food Quality Protection Act of 1996; the bad news is that the process is slow, leaving millions of children jeopardized in the meantime.

Another outspoken and highly credible consumer watchdog group, Consumers Union (CU), publishers of *Consumer Reports,* has researched pesticide residues and other forms of unlabeled food contamination, such as transgenic ingredients. CU analyzed the results of Department of Agriculture sample testing between 1994 and 1997 on twenty-seven food categories. In all, CU interpreted toxicity data for 27,000 samples at about 5 pounds of produce each. "Of the 27 foods the USDA tested in the four years we analyzed, seven—apples, grapes, green beans, peaches, pears, spinach, and winter squash—stand out as having a toxicity score up to hundreds of times higher than the rest."[18]

While the report goes on to explain that toxicity levels don't necessarily mean that a food is unsafe, it cautions that children are at special risk for the reasons already specified—greater neurological and developmental vulnerability and the likelihood that children will eat far more of some foods, such as peaches, per pound of body weight than adults, making it easy for children to take in toxic doses in a short period of time. What about spinach, the green food that evokes cheers when we see children eating it? According to the CU report, "One in 13 spinach samples had pesticide residues that were over the safe daily limit for a 44-pound child eating a single serving. The USDA tests also found more illegal pesticides on spinach—15 in all—than on any other crop." And Consumer Union's recommendation? Wash vegetables very thoroughly— "or consider buying organic."[19]

In addition to Environmental Working Group and Consumers Union, other groups, including Beyond Pesticides (formerly National Coalition Against the Misuse of Pesticides), Mothers & Others for a Livable Planet,

Natural Resources Defense Council, Union of Concerned Scientists, Environmental Defense, and Pesticide Action Network of North America (PANNA), have also done illuminating and courageous work to educate consumers about the real dangers of pesticides. (These groups and more are listed in this book's Resources section.)

PROGRESS OF A SORT:
THE FOOD QUALITY PROTECTION ACT

In the face of undeniable evidence that pesticide tolerance levels had been set by the EPA with inadequate information and testing protocols in place, the Food Quality Protection Act (FQPA) was signed into law in 1996 with overwhelming approval from the House and Senate. FQPA requires that pesticides must be evaluated or reevaluated for safety when infants and children are exposed. Under the law, allowances must be made for children's greater vulnerability to damage from such exposure; risk evaluation must incorporate the potential for increased threats as a result of the organism's exposure to multiple chemicals; and food company profits as a result of using a given pesticide must carry significantly less weight in the risk equation.

The Food Quality Protection Act is a powerful improvement over old laws that required no explicit protection of infants and children in assessing risk. But so far, little progress has been made to implement its edicts. Environmental groups have begun to assume a fatalistic approach to pesticide risk reassessment, recommending that concerned citizens act as if little, if anything, will be done by government to remove dangerous agricultural chemicals from the market or to meaningfully reduce allowable limits. Loopholes, tremendous pressure from powerful pesticide lobbies, and a simple failure to progress are all to blame.

The group of pesticides known as organophosphates, which the EPA said would be the first to be revisited under FQPA, remain an insidious threat to children's health. Every day, according to government data, more than 1 million children age five and under eat an unsafe dose of organophosphate insecticides, and 100,000 of these children significantly exceed the EPA "safe dose."[20]

The law permits the EPA to act, but unless weaknesses in FQPA and the implementation process are corrected, the agency may not do so with the urgency that the dangers of pesticides require. Again, the burden falls to the consumer. Arm yourself with knowledge, with information, with a refusal to be "spun" by chemical company public relations machines. And make choices in the way you eat and the way your children eat that reflect your concerns and your expectations for safe food and full disclosure of the risks of that food.

PESTICIDE EXPOSURE IN HOMES AND SCHOOLS

The Environmental Protection Agency recently did take some action on one of the potent organophosphate pesticides. The restrictions the EPA placed beginning June 8, 2000, on the use of Dursban, or chlorpyrifos, are an unfortunate reminder of the many sources of exposure to these chemicals. The agency, responding to research assessing the real toxicity of chlorpyrifos, one of the most commonly used pesticides in America, placed few additional restrictions on its widespread agricultural use. But the EPA banned over-the-counter sales of Dursban and other chlorpyrifos home and garden products (though it did not ask that products currently on store shelves be pulled) and prohibited its use in schools, day care centers, shopping centers, and other structures. Some professional uses, including at golf courses, are still allowed. The EPA will also allow manufacturers to continue to make and export chlorpyrifos. More than 11 million pounds of chlorpyrifos are used annually in homes and gardens.[21]

Many concerned citizens and environmental groups feel that the EPA has not gone far enough; they want a complete ban of Dursban and other organophosphates. Consumers should avoid all products containing this chemical. But heed the lesson: Once again, a product that the government claimed safe for use in our homes, day care centers, and schools for more than twenty years has now been shown, by the government's own admission, to be a clear and present danger to the health of small children and pets.

If you are concerned about the risks of pesticides to infants and children, you must look beyond food. Lawn and garden chemicals, home insecticides, and chemicals used in schools to control pests are all very consequential sources of exposure. Look at what's in your garden shed or what your lawn company and exterminators are using. Take steps to minimize your family's exposure.

Find out what chemicals your child's school uses. If there are farms nearby, find out what chemicals they're using. Do your homework on the potential dangers of these chemicals, and consider the worst: What if they're about to join the long list of chemicals that were once believed to be safe and are now, evidently, not? You can't control everything, and you risk disdain and even anger by voicing your concerns. But you may also find that by joining with others in the community to ask questions and investigate alternatives, you can effect change. Adults, to some extent, can choose their poisons, but children deserve full protection from potential risk. Chemicals should be proved safe before use, not used until proved harmful, and the burden of that proof of safety should be on the companies that wish to profit from manufacturing and distributing these products.

One scientist who has expressed this in a truly eloquent and poignant way is Sandra Steingraber, author of *Living Downstream: A Scientist's Personal Investigation of Cancer and the Environment.* I highly recommend this book to anyone who has even the slightest concern about environmental toxins. To call it eye-opening and moving is an understatement. Steingraber gives us three key principles by which to test the legitimacy of our use of chemicals that affect public health. These are quite different, as you'll see, from the way business and government currently make these decisions:

> One [key principle] is the idea that public and private interests should act to prevent harm before it occurs. This is known as the *precautionary principle,* and it dictates that indication of harm, rather than proof of harm, should be the trigger for action—especially if delay may cause irreparable damage. Central to the precautionary principle is the recognition that we have an obligation to protect human life. Our current methods of regulation, by contrast, appear governed by what some frustrated policymakers have called the dead body approach: Wait until damage is proven before action is taken. It is a system tantamount to running an uncontrolled experiment using human subjects.

Closely related to the precautionary principle is the *principle of reverse onus*. According to this edict, it is safety, rather than harm, that should necessitate demonstration. This reversal essentially shifts the burden of proof off the shoulders of the public and onto those who produce, import, or use the substance in question. The principle of reverse onus requires that those who seek to introduce chemicals into our environment first show that what they propose to do is almost certainly *not* going to hurt anyone. This is already the standard we uphold for pharmaceuticals, and yet for most industrial chemicals, no firm requirement for advance demonstration of safety exists. But chemicals are not citizens. They should not be presumed innocent unless proven guilty, especially when a verdict of guilt requires some of us to sicken and die in order to demonstrate the necessary evidence.

Finally, all activities with potential public health consequences should be guided by the *principle of the least toxic alternative,* which presumes that toxic substances will not be used as long as there is another way of accomplishing the task. This means choosing the least harmful way of solving problems—whether it be ridding fields of weeds, school cafeterias of cockroaches, dogs of fleas, woolens of stains, or drinking water of pathogens.[22]

The world our children will inherit will look very different if these kinds of principles are introduced and embraced. A true vision of sustainability—a concept that suggests that we will leave our children a livable world without depleted resources—demands that we approach chemical applications in this way. In the meantime, clearly the world our children inhabit today must be carefully monitored for their protection.

A NOTE ABOUT
FARMWORKERS' CHILDREN

When making choices about supporting organic agriculture and buying organic foods, it's important that we consider the children of farmworkers as well as our own families. Children living in agricultural communities where conventional agriculture is practiced often show even higher levels of toxins at possibly unsafe levels in their bodies.[23, 24] These same children

Environmental Working Group and FoodNews.org

Environmental Working Group (EWG) is a Washington-based non-profit "content provider for public interest groups and concerned citizens who are campaigning to protect the environment."[25] Founded in 1993, EWG has done important research and dissemination of information about pesticides and chemicals and, specifically, the impact of environmental toxins on infants and children. A staff of eighteen researchers, computer experts, and writers produce reports and other material as comprehensive and credible as it is accessible and valuable. Their award-winning Web site at www.ewg.org is easy to navigate and well worth frequent visits.

The EWG project FoodNews.org is one of my favorite ways to show people the realities of pesticide residues in a way that's interactive, fun, yet educational. Are you interested in getting a graphic, vivid picture of the pesticides you and your family might be ingesting every day, based on tens of thousands of food samples tested by the government? Pay a visit to www.food-news.org and just enter your choices, from the meal you just finished to the fruit salad of your dreams. The interactive simulator randomly picks samples for the foods you choose from a database with "results of more than 90,000 government lab tests for food contaminants," the site says.

You can enter just one food or a whole day's worth; you can specify kids' diets or create a virtual fruit salad and check it for chemicals. Because the site's computer picks its government data at random, the same meal might reveal few pesticide residues one day and dozens the next, just as residues vary at the supermarket.

After the site tells you how many pesticides you've just eaten in cyberspace, it'll tell you their documented health risks and how frequently you've ingested them. By clicking on a chemical name, you can go one step further and learn technical information about the substance.

One of the site's options lets you measure the pesticide risk from eating "an apple a day," the folk remedy for health, for a year. I tried this option on May 31, 2000, and got the following results: By eating an apple a day for a year (conventionally grown, washed and cored), I ingested thirty-eight different pesticides, with health risks that included cancer, birth defects, damage to the reproductive system, interference with hormones, damage to the brain and nervous system, and damage to the immune system. On any given day, I had a better chance of consuming an apple with seven or more pesticides than an apple with no pesticides, according to foodnews.org.

It's a fun interactive site with a disturbing message: The food supply is indeed full of contamination. Because we don't know the real risks of cumulative exposure to multiple pesticides, our bodies and future generations are the laboratory for the many chemicals we're exposed to every day. And all the data on residues and health effects come from the same agencies that tell us not to worry. EWG's number 1 recommendation? *"Buy as much organic food as possible* [italics mine] or shop for foods that are certified as low in pesticides, like Kashi cereals or NutriClean produce."

sometimes do not have access to adequate health care. They are truly innocent bystanders in a world of chemicals that may limit healthy development. Supporting organic means helping to create increasing opportunities for workers on organic farms, where there is much less exposure to toxins.

SUMMARY

- Children at rapid stages of development are likely to be harmed by pesticide exposure more than fully grown adults.
- Children's diets tend to include more foods likely to be contaminated with pesticide residues.
- Pesticide tolerance levels have been set for adult males and single exposures, rather than small children who often experience exposure to multiple chemicals simultaneously.

- Residue tolerances long considered safe must now be reviewed, and under this scrutiny, "safe" levels are proving to be unsafe for children.
- Children also suffer exposure in homes and schools and on lawns.
- Infant formula and baby foods may have pesticide residues and genetically modified ingredients.
- Even breast milk carries a toxic burden, making protecting children from unnecessary additional exposure even more important.

Conclusion

It may seem odd to come to the end of a book about organic foods with no recipes, no way to tell you how to cook them. One of your questions about organic foods may be, "How do I cook them?" The answer is, just like other foods. The range of organic foods available is so wide, the quality generally so high, you'll find that whatever dishes you create will be better. You can mix all the organic and nonorganic foods you like, though hopefully, that's not happening to fresh food in the marketplace. Of course, I hope you will incorporate the idea of eating fresh, seasonal foods and not confine your organic experience to snack foods. But all in all, this is a book about how organic food is grown. I hope it will add a new dimension, a sense of awareness, to everything you cook and eat.

Understanding organic agriculture and its purpose lets us begin to build a new relationship with food and farms. And once we've renewed our sense of where food comes from, the options seem to multiply to make connections and create community through food. At first, though, from the discomfort of learning what pesticides really can do to children's health to really learning to differentiate the kinds of food production processes reflected in the marketplace, it can seem like hard work.

But being an informed food consumer doesn't mean that all the fun goes out of eating. In fact, the greatest pleasures can begin when we know the source of our foods. The experience of food changes for the better when we get closer to the source.

Supporting organic means enjoying delicious food that's been guided from field to table with a sense of ecological responsibility. It means expanding our communities to include farms once again. For many chefs, it means revising perceptions of what gourmet food can be and introducing diners to a new and creative cuisine based on fresh and seasonal produce.

Some of these chefs, like Jesse Cool of Flea Street Cafe in Menlo Park, California, and Nora Pouillon of Nora's Restaurant in Washington, D.C., are expanding the boundaries of sustainable agriculture to sustainable cuisine, where every aspect of restaurant service and food preparation uses ecological and humane principles. Restaurants are creating innovative partnerships with farms, ensuring fresh supplies for the chefs and support for the growers. A group of innovative restaurateurs and chefs called Chefs Collaborative 2000 has led this movement (see Resources).

So organic farmers, hand in hand with consumers, are changing the way food is grown, changing the way we look at food and how we eat, and now changing the way we dine out. All of these things enrich our communities. I believe that the organic movement is also revitalizing gardening—not just in home gardens, which are one of the very best ways to connect to the source of food, but school gardens, community gardens, urban gardens, therapeutic gardens, meditation gardens, prison gardens, gardens designed for the disabled, and even homeless gardens. Growing food, as our most fundamental connection with the earth, then blossoms into a means to connect with others and with ourselves.

School gardens also offer phenomenal educational opportunities. Alice Waters, of Chez Panisse Restaurant fame, has been quoted as saying, "The most neglected schoolroom is the lunchroom." To help educate children about growing food, she's instituted a program called the Edible Schoolyard to develop organic gardens in more schools. The garden becomes a living workshop for biology, chemistry, art, and botany; it can be written about, discussed, and planned.

At the Asilomar Ecological Farming Conference a few years ago, I heard a woman talk about an impressive project. I don't remember her name, but the vision and spirit of this exercise was inspiring. She had helped organize a class in a middle school in what I believe was a not-too-affluent district. The students planted an organic garden, nourished and cultivated it, harvested the yield, then planned and created a meal from the produce. They then took the meal to a local shelter and served the meal themselves to those in the shelter. I suspect that the learning that took place during the course of the project was multidimensional and long-lasting for these remarkable children.

The same spirit of connectedness can infuse all kinds of gardens in every kind of community. Home gardens, too, can be rewarding at any size, not to mention educational and economical. Nature gives us a living laboratory to learn about sustainability and ecology in our own backyard or even in our own windowsill herb garden.

EATING RESPONSIBLY

Eating in the modern world is a political act. "The personal is political" was one of the catchphrases of the 1960s, applied to everything from the feminist movement to civil rights and antiwar sentiment. To me, that phrase meant that every act mattered and we had a responsibility to understand how it mattered; for example, it finally sank in for me that a cigarette habit was not the act of a progressive rebel but an act in support, however tacitly, of tobacco companies and those who profited from them. Individual choices do matter.

If eating has never seemed to you like a lofty enough act to earn the same scrutiny, the same measure of acting with integrity, I hope this book has changed your mind. The food we eat every day is our closest relationship to the natural world. Food is the source of our lives and our health. Yet the conventional food system in this country has taken us in a direction that has nearly severed this connection and our understanding of food. Our control over how food is grown and produced has been abdicated to chemical companies and factory farming. Our connection to farms as the source of our food supply is remote (if it exists at all). We do battle with weight and body image, see food as the enemy, and embrace diets that hurt our health, make us fat, increase our risk of cancer and heart disease, and lead us to ever more artificial forms of "diet" food when fat starts to win the war.

Though I believe with all my heart in organic agriculture and natural foods, I am not a "health food fascist." I am not a vegetarian, and I am not a farmer. I've never even learned to be a very good cook. But I have learned that understanding where food comes from and how it's grown, processed, and manufactured matters. And in some ways, it is those of us who don't have a perfect diet, who indulge ourselves perhaps too often, and who aren't perfect cooks who most need high-quality food grown with a heart and soul and a connection to the earth and the cycles of life.

The price of a food system that degrades our environment and threatens the health of future generations is much too high. Food grown with the principles of ecological wholeness, diversity, and protection and humane treatment for all forms of life is the only option we can afford.

An Organic Farmer Looks at the Future

This sourcebook marks a watershed in the history of the organic foods movement. For the first time, there is now an authoritative information resource on organic foods for both consumers and analysts of the movement. It is, in a sense, a portrait of the movement's cumulative identity that is honest and accurate, and, like the best paintings, provides insights not available from an ordinary snapshot.

It is also a portrait of a subject still in relative infancy, with all the great potential this implies. This book allows us some perspective on the movement as a whole and shows how far we've come. But we still have so much to discover about how to have a bountiful agricultural system for everybody, without destruction of the land or its keepers. What will this portrait look like in five or ten years?

First, the picture will be much bigger. With the implementation of national standards, we will see the growth of existing markets and the development of new markets. New production and manufactured products will continue to proliferate, bringing an ever-wider assortment of organically produced goods to more people. There will be increasing international trade in all types of organic foods.

However, this growth will bring both opportunity and peril for organic family farmers. There will be great opportunity to tap new markets, but the inevitable trend of consolidation in the retail and distribution sectors will put pressure on smaller-scale producers.

This is the great dilemma for all of farming in the early twenty-first century. Organic production does not automatically provide a solution, but the organic imperative to understand the whole system and encompass all the dimensions of production creates an awareness that is essential to finding an answer. And industrialized, genetically engineered agriculture will become an even more dramatic background, a stark contrast to the growing organic sector. The massive forces guiding the dominant vision of agriculture may encounter obstacles (such as the fiasco with Starlink genetically engineered corn in late 2000), but they won't be derailed. Too much has been invested by too many for these tools to simply be set aside until we are wise enough to use them safely. The trend toward fewer, more gigantic factory farms will probably also continue to accelerate, with dire consequences for the rural population and its landscape.

Against this background, organic agriculture now offers at least the possibility of an alternative vision. A decade from now, we hope that the organic portrait will still include the substance and depth of this vision. It is possible that the organic movement can help to steer the awesome power of genetic engineering and other technologies in the direction of sustainable systems, and do so on a broad scale. If this happens, it will be in the context of a significant new investment in organic farming research and development. This is potentially the most important development of all, with benefits far beyond the organic community. The scientific frontier of organic agriculture is still virtually unexplored. Our ability to develop nontoxic, high-yielding systems will steadily increase, at a rate that is determined by the resources our society is willing to put into this effort.

The development of such systems, and their widespread adoption throughout the farm community, might even create a situation where the term *organic* becomes redundant. This point might perhaps be twenty or fifty years into the future, but the astonishing growth and acceptance of organic foods in the last ten years should caution us not to make too many assumptions about how fast things can change.

Making beneficial change is ultimately the moral of this story, the real implication of this sourcebook. If there is one thing the reader should take away, it is that we all have the power to create change that is felt at the highest levels. We do it with our choices every day and by sticking with those choices over the long haul. The details of the organic portrait will change with time, but we must all remain dedicated to the vision of a better, healthier way to feed ourselves and live on this planet.

MARK LIPSON
Policy program director
Organic Farming Research Foundation
Santa Cruz, California
He has been farming organically since 1983.

Resources

ALL-STAR ORGANIZATIONS

These are nonprofit and trade organizations doing important work with a focus on organic agriculture, environmental protection, or food. Each has a different mission, but all share a zeal to inform, educate, innovate, and provide alternatives and choices.

These are just a few excellent places to start. There are many other effective and noteworthy organizations doing this work. You'll find additional organizations, publications, and Web sites elsewhere in this Resources section, and most of these can lead you to many more options through links on the Internet or other means.

Organic Trade Association (OTA)
www.ota.com
74 Fairview Street
P.O. Box 547
Greenfield, MA 01302
(413) 774-7511
E-mail: info@ota.com

The Organic Trade Association serves the needs and interests of member companies engaged in commerce, but also provides good essential information about organics and speaks out to the media on behalf of organics. OTA's Web site is the place to start for statistics about the growing organic market, for information on selling organic goods in retail outlets, and other information about the marketplace. If you're even thinking about including organics in your business, consider joining OTA.

Organic Farming Research Foundation (OFRF)
www.ofrf.org
P.O. Box 440
Santa Cruz, CA 95061
(831) 426-6606
E-mail: research@ofrf.org

OFRF's mission is to sponsor research related to organic farming practices, to disseminate research results to organic farmers and to growers interested in adopting organic production systems, and to educate the public and decision makers about organic farming issues. In the absence of any support—to understate the situation— from traditional institutions for organic farming research, the OFRF team not only created a foundation to fund on-farm organic research, but has taken their case to Washington and fought hard for federal recognition and a share of our tax dollars for organic farming research. The battle goes on, though, and OFRF needs and deserves support. Visit www.ofrf.org to learn more.

Organic Alliance
www.organic.org
400 Selby Avenue, Suite T
St. Paul, MN 55102

Organic Alliance is a nonprofit organization whose mission is "to encourage an ecologically and socially responsible agriculture which reflects humankind's obligation to protect the health of the planet for future generations." To this end, the Alliance works with farmers, processors, distributors, retailers, and consumers. Recently, one focus has been educating conventional supermarket personnel about the why and how of offering the organic choice to consumers.

Farm Aid
www.farmaid.org
11 Ward Street, Suite 200
Somerville, MA 02143
(617) 354-2922

Farm Aid is well known as an annual outdoor music extrava-
ganza headlined by founders Willie Nelson, Neil Young, and John
Mellencamp, but it's also a year-round nonprofit organization dedicated to helping save family farms. They've raised and distributed
millions of dollars, but it's hard to stem the tide and restore the
damage done by industrial agriculture. Help them out: Buy the
Farm Aid CD (from Best Buy's Redline Entertainment), make a
donation, purchase a concert ticket or a T-shirt, and read what they
have to say at www.farmaid.org.

Chefs Collaborative
www.chefnet.com/cc2000
441 Stuart Street, Suite 712
Boston, MA 02116
(617) 236-5200
E-mail: cc2000@chefnet.com

Chefs Collaborative is "a network of chefs and members of the
food community across the United States who promote sustainable
cuisine by teaching children, supporting local farmers, educating
each other, and inspiring their customers to choose clean, healthy
foods." If you're a "foodie" who loves the idea of world-class
gourmet food grown with sustainable roots, or if you're a food
professional with an interest in sustainable cuisine, join Chefs
Collaborative. You'll be in good company, with chefs Rick Bayless,
Nora Pouillon, Jesse Cool, and many more. Local chapters host regular events and may join the Adopt-a-School program that teaches
kids about global and sustainable cuisine. A national newsletter
provides updates and valuable information for advocates of healthy

and environmentally sound foods. Anyone who supports the Collaborative's mission can join; at the very least, find out which chefs in your community are members of Chefs Collaborative, and support them enthusiastically.

Pesticide Action Network of North America (PANNA)
www.panna.org
49 Powell Street, Suite 500
San Francisco, CA 94102
(415) 981-1771
E-mail: panna@panna.org

Since 1982, PANNA has worked to help eliminate toxic pesticides from the environment. Pesticide Action Network is actually a global network for international pesticide reform, with PANNA as the North American branch. PANNA provides research and education updates on a number of pesticide-related issues as well as a database for pesticide toxicity and regulatory information. PANNA provides accessible yet comprehensive information, guidelines for action, and information about pesticides in the home, garden, and food supply, along with product and exposure information. California residents may be especially interested in PANNA's data on pesticide use in that state (total pesticide use in 1998 was the highest level ever reported up to then, they say).

Beyond Pesticides/National Coalition
Against the Misuse of Pesticides (NCAMP)
www.beyondpesticides.org
701 E Street SE, Suite 200
Washington, DC 20003
(202) 543-4791
E-mail: info@beyondpesticides.org

Beyond Pesticides, formerly known as NCAMP, began in 1981 to serve as a national network seeking to focus public attention on pesticide risks and less toxic alternatives. They're an excellent resource for information about nonagricultural uses of pesticides, including chemical treatment of wood utility poles, mosquito spraying in densely populated areas, and pesticide use in schools and public buildings.

Environmental Defense (ED)
(Formerly Environmental Defense Fund/EDF)
www.environmentaldefense.org
257 Park Avenue South
New York, NY 10010
1-800-684-3322 (membership)

Environmental Defense, formerly Environmental Defense Fund, is a nonprofit organization with more than three hundred thousand members that has, since 1967, "linked science, economics, and law to create innovative, equitable, and cost-effective solutions to the most urgent environmental problems." ED was founded to work for a ban on DDT, a pesticide banned in this country in 1972. Since then, ED has involved itself in a broad range of issues. They have excellent information on the health of the oceans and fish populations, global warming, and more. Their home Web site will lead you to sites for specific projects, including Scorecard, which monitors corporate pollution nationwide, and the eye-opening Hog Watch, which tracks pollution from factory hog farming.

Environmental Working Group (EWG)
www.ewg.org
1718 Connecticut Avenue NW, Suite 600
Washington, DC 20009
E-mail: info@ewg.org

Environmental Working Group describes itself as "an environmental and public health watchdog group that conducts computer investigations into the toxins in food, air, and water—as well as the influence peddling that worsens these problems. EWG's mission is to equip people with information so they can be engaged environmental citizens." And inform us EWG does, with some of the most valuable, well-founded, take-no-prisoners information about toxins available anywhere. Their work on pesticides and children was essential to the writing of this book. As a content provider to public interest groups and consumers, all of EWG's reports and Web sites are invaluable, and whenever someone needs a highly graphic, visual, entertaining, eye-opening look at pesticides in foods, I send them straight to www.foodnews.org, an EWG site, to make a little fruit salad. Try it.

Union of Concerned Scientists (UCS)

www.ucsusa.org
2 Brattle Square
Cambridge, MA 02238
(617) 547-5552
E-mail: ucs@ucsusa.org

Union of Concerned Scientists is an independent, nonprofit alliance of fifty thousand citizens and scientists. The organization was founded in 1969 by faculty and students at Massachusetts Institute of Technology. As change advocates and scientific experts, they form a highly credible and authoritative voice on a wide range of environmental issues. For the purposes of this book, I want to especially note their work in evaluating transgenic technologies and their potential risks. Margaret Mellon, UCS's agriculture and biotechnology program director, coauthored *Ecological Risks of Engineered Crops* (MIT Press, 1996), a rigorous technical analysis.

For the nonscientist, UCS has put together *The Consumer's Guide to Effective Environmental Choices: Practical Advice from the Union of Concerned Scientists,* by Michael Brower, Ph.D., and Warren Leon, Ph.D. (Three Rivers Press, 1999), full of excellent, practical, well-researched advice about everyday choices. They show us that some of the decisions we sweat over are nearly moot; choosing between paper and plastic bags at the grocery store, for example, is inconsequential (they're almost equal in their environmental costs; bring your own cloth bag to make a difference) compared to deciding how to get there—driving alone in an SUV to that same store, say, versus walking, taking public transportation, or sharing a ride.

Center for Science in the Public Interest (CSPI)
www.cspinet.org
1875 Connecticut Avenue NW, Suite 300
Washington, DC 20009
(202) 332-9110
E-mail: cspi@cspinet.org

CSPI is a watchdog organization for the food industry. A nonprofit organization funded in part by subscriptions to its well-known newsletter, *Nutrition Action Healthletter,* CSPI says it "seeks to promote health through educating the public about nutrition and alcohol; it represents citizens' interests before legislative, regulatory, and judicial bodies; and it works to ensure advances in science are used for the public good." Like Consumers Union, CSPI offers straightforward, independent, and credible analyses of claims that affect consumers. CSPI has been a strong voice for limits on antibiotic use in poultry and has published succinct reports examining the real nutritional value of many foods. Junk foods, fast foods, sodas, and other foods with little nutritional value have all come under their microscope. They also offer great advice about food safety practices, evaluate new products, and make recommendations about diets and food groups.

Turning Point Project
www.turnpoint.org
666 Pennsylvania Avenue SE, Suite 302
Washington, DC 20003
1-800-249-8712
E-mail: info@turnpoint.org

The Turning Point Project is a nonprofit organization formed in 1999 specifically to design and produce a series of educational advertisements concerning major environmental issues of the new millennium, including industrial agriculture, genetic engineering, and the global extinction crisis. Turning Point's educational advertisements run in the *New York Times* and are also available in print and on their Web site as educational booklets with excellent, extensive resource lists. Each ad is signed by members of a coalition of more than eighty environmental and social nonprofit groups.

Community Food Security Coalition (CFSC)
www.foodsecurity.org
P.O. Box 209
Venice, CA 90294
(310) 822-5410
E-mail: info@foodsecurity.org

If you're interested in the concept of food security—communities having some control over their own food supply—this is a good place to start. CFSC's work is a reminder that hunger is still an issue in this country and that everyone deserves safe, high-quality food. CFSC is a nonprofit, membership-based coalition of more than six hundred organizations and individuals. Their mission, CFSC says, is to bring about lasting social change by promoting community-based solutions to hunger, poor nutrition, and the globalization of the food system.

ORGANIC COMPANY WEB SITES AND GENERAL DIRECTORIES

There are thousands of companies involved in the organic foods and fiber marketplace. (It's a wonderful measure of the success of organic foods.) My intent here is not to promote one company over another, but to mention a few national companies that are doing a great job of helping to educate the organic consumer. It's important, I believe, to buy local whenever you can, but we're lucky to have these national brands, too, and each of them has good information about organic agriculture and production on its Web site.

Both the Organic Trade Association and the Community Alliance of Family Farmers publish annual directories that include growers, manufacturers, distributors, brokers, support companies, and more if you're in search of more complete guides to the full spectrum of organic businesses. Those directories are listed here as well. I've also included a few Web sites that offer on-line organic shopping or links to companies, farms, and restaurants.

Newman's Own Organics

www.newmansownorganics.com

This division of Newman's Own, started by Nell Newman, makes only organic foods—pretzels, cookies, chocolate bars, and amazing organic peanut butter cups. They share a commitment to social service with Newman's Own and donate *all profits* to charitable causes.

Stonyfield Farm

www.stonyfield.com

Stonyfield Farm makes organic and natural yogurt and ice cream. They've made their mark as a company that supports organic farming and has pioneered new standards for socially and environmentally responsible business. Look for their free guides on global warming and organic foods.

Organic Valley Family of Farms

www.organicvalley.com

A farmers cooperative based in Wisconsin that sells dairy products, meat, and eggs, this cooperative began in 1988 with

7 members and has grown to 160 members and a nationally recognized brand.

Lundberg Family Farms
www.lundberg.com

Generations of Lundbergs have farmed rice in California's Sacramento Valley since 1937. Today they offer organic rice and "nutra-farmed" products (check the packages for information about Lundberg's nutra-farming methods). Conventional rice growers burn the rice fields, pouring smoke filled with particles that can harm human lungs into the air. Organic rice avoids this danger and protects wetlands habitats as well. Visit the Web site for recipes, mail-order options, and a newsletter.

Earthbound Farm
www.ebfarm.com

Earthbound Farm, under parent company Natural Selection Foods, is one of the nation's largest packagers of organic lettuce and salad mixes. You'll also see the label on cherry tomatoes and heirloom tomatoes. In Carmel, California, you can visit their lovely farm stand on the land where the company began. Earthbound Farm organic produce is easy to find in conventional supermarkets as well as natural markets.

Pavich Family Farm
www.pavich.com

A large California-based grower of organic produce, Pavich is probably best known for delicious table grapes and for tins of huge, plump, organic raisins that kids love. Pavich is widely available in conventional as well as natural supermarkets.

Small Planet Foods
www.smallplanetfoods.com

Small Planet Foods is the parent company for Muir Glen, a line of great canned organic tomato products, and Cascadian Farm, best known for organic frozen vegetables and convenience foods. They're now owned by General Mills but say they're able to maintain their long-standing commitment to organic advocacy and small farmers.

Horizon Organics
www.horizonorganic.com

Horizon makes organic milk, dairy products, citrus juices, and more. They've expanded rapidly into conventional markets and overseas. Of special interest: the Horizon Organic Dairy, Farm & Education Center, a multimedia educational center on a former naval dairy in Maryland. If you'd like to visit the center, see Horizon's Web site for details.

Web sites

Organic Kitchen.com
www.organickitchen.com

Links to foods, restaurants, farms, markets, vineyards, cooking, gardening, and organic living.

Organic Growers Web Site
www.organic-growers.com

If you can't get to a farm, take a virtual tour through the links on the Organic-Growers.com Growers' Index, connecting you to farms all over the world. The Resource Links page takes you to all kinds of organic and environmental organizations, and there's more.

OrganicInfo.com
www.organicinfo.com

An advertising-supported site, otherwise unaffiliated with any organic company, offering general information and many links to consumer groups, environmental organizations, organic companies, farms, and more.

Eco-Organics
www.eco-organics.com

On-line organic and health foods grocery, with organic fruits, vegetables, breads, groceries, "eco-fashion," gift baskets, and more.

General Directories

National Organic Directory: An International Guide to Organic Information and Resources, 17th ed. (Davis, Calif.: Community Alliance with Family Farmers, 2000).

Growers, companies, resources, and current articles by experts in the organic field. To purchase, contact Community Alliance with Family Farmers, by E-mail at nod@caff.org, call 1-800-852-3832, or visit www.caff.org.

The Organic Pages: Organic Trade Association's North American Resource Directory (New York: Succotash Press, 1998).

Annual directory with listings of OTA members, including growers, companies, support organizations, and retailers. To purchase, contact Organic Trade Association by E-mail at info@ota.com, call

(413) 774-7511, or visit www.ota.com, where *The Organic Pages* is also available on-line.

RECOMMENDED READING: COMMUNITY AND PHILOSOPHY

These are some favorite books on the land, food, and the environment, as well as periodicals that often cover issues related to organic foods, sustainable agriculture, and community.

Books

Rachel Carson, *Silent Spring* (New York: Houghton Mifflin, 1962). Introduction by Al Gore, 1994.

The book that began a movement, still worth reading for its passionate, courageous analysis of a world-changing technology.

Wendell Berry, *What Are People For?* (New York: North Point Press, 1990).

Wendell Berry is a brilliant writer, poet, and farmer and a former professor at the University of Kentucky. Berry has become one of the most eminent voices of our time, writing about the importance of local and rural communities, true conservation, the pleasures of eating and food, and more.

Wendell Berry, *Another Turn of the Crank* (Washington, D.C.: Counterpoint, 1995).

Another set of six essays by Berry—a provocative and worthwhile treasure.

David Mas Masumoto, *Epitaph for a Peach: Four Seasons on My Family Farm* (San Francisco: HarperCollins, 1995).

An eloquent journey through a year of peach farming by a small farmer and a wonderful writer.

Victor Davis Hanson, *Fields Without Dreams: Defending the Agrarian Idea* (New York: Free Press, 1996).

Hanson, a California farmer and a scholar (he is a professor of Greek at a California State University), examines both our myths and truths about farming.

Victor Davis Hanson, *The Land Was Everything: Letters from an American Farmer* (New York: Free Press, 2000).

Hanson hits hard, again, on our myths and beliefs about farming, nature, and rural communities.

Wes Jackson, *Becoming Native to This Place* (Washington, D.C.: Counterpoint, 1994, 1996).

Jackson is the founder of the Land Institute, a Salina, Kansas, nonprofit environmental organization. His thoughtful discourse on farming and the land comes from both a scientific and an environmental perspective.

Paul Hawken, *The Ecology of Commerce: A Declaration of Sustainability* (New York: HarperCollins, 1993).

Hawken, the founder of Smith & Hawken, describes his vision of sustainable and responsible business, with some attention to agriculture and food.

Earth Pledge Foundation, *Sustainable Cuisine White Papers* (New York: Earth Pledge Foundation, 1999).

This lovely collection of essays on sustainable cuisine is available in its entirety on the Internet at www.earthpledge.org, or contact Earth Pledge, 485 Madison Avenue, 24th Floor, New York, NY 10022, (212) 688-2216.

Periodicals

Whole Earth
www.wholeearthmag.com
Subscriptions 1-888-732-6739

This magazine has all the principles, quality, and elegance of its parent publication, the original *Whole Earth Catalog,* in a very relevant quarterly publication for today.

Orion and Orion Afield
www.orionsociety.org

Both are publications of the Orion Society, an environmental action group supporting "place-based environmentalism" with a grassroots network of activist nonprofits around the country.

Food & Water Journal
www.foodandwater.org

The journal of Food & Water, a political action organization dedicated to local, safe, and sustainable alternatives in food production.

Utne Reader
www.utne.com

"The best of the alternative media" and more. Always interesting and provocative.

WorldWatch
www.worldwatch.org

The journal of the Worldwatch Institute, a Washington-based nonprofit public policy research organization focused on links between economic and enviromental issues globally.

The Ecologist
www.theecologist.org

The Ecologist is the world's longest-running magazine.

CHEFS, COOKBOOKS, AND CULINARY ORGANIZATIONS

Food lovers can find many wonderful cookbooks by chefs who support sustainable agriculture and who use organic and locally grown ingredients. While any recipe can be made using organic foods, these chefs are not only extraordinarily talented but inspiring when it comes to a focus on freshness, quality, and knowing where your ingredients come from.

The books, periodicals, and resources that follow are just a few of my favorites, but I encourage you to also explore the work of such chefs as Rick Bayless, Nora Pouillon, Mollie Katzen, Deborah Madison, Charlie Trotter, Annemarie Colbin, and Annie Somerville. Don't forget local newspapers and the national editions of the *New York Times* and the *Los Angeles Times,* whose Wednesday food sections often include coverage of organic foods and recipes by organic-minded chefs and culinary experts.

Books

Jesse Cool, *Your Organic Kitchen* (Emmaus, Penn.: Rodale Press, 2000).

Jesse Cool, founder of Flea Street Cafe and JZCOOL restaurants in Menlo Park, California, is truly a chef who feeds the heart and soul as well as the body. Along with great, easy-to-follow recipes, this lovely book also has lots of good information about organics.

Alice Waters et al., *Chez Panisse Cafe Cookbook* (New York: Harper-Collins, 1999).

Alice Waters is an extraordinary chef and food activist who pioneered the concept of local, regional, fresh food as the pinnacle of what "gourmet" can mean. Waters has championed organic foods and farming and more recently has begun a campaign for gardens and quality food in the schools, saying, "The most neglected schoolroom is the lunchroom." These recipes come from the kitchen of Chez Panisse, Waters's famed Berkeley, California, restaurant. Some recipes in this beautiful book call for unusual ingredients; if you have good local markets and an adventurous nature, give it a try. Also recommended: *Chez Panisse Vegetables, Chez Panisse Desserts,* and other books by Waters.

John Ash with Sid Goldstein, *From the Earth to the Table* (New York: Dutton, 1995).

Ash is a well-known wine country chef. This book reflects his work as the chef at Fetzer Vineyards in Mendocino County in California. Stellar California cuisine for those who love to cook.

Annie Somerville, *Fields of Greens: New Vegetarian Recipes from the Celebrated Greens Restaurant* (New York: Bantam Books, 1993).

These are lovely, complex, sophisticated vegetarian recipes with seasonal flavor from a pioneer in the world of natural and vegetarian cooking.

Fran McManus, ed., *Cooking Fresh from the Bay Area* (San Diego: Eating Fresh Publications, 2000).

It's no surprise that so much good food made with organic ingredients comes from the Bay Area, where so much that is innovative in both food and agriculture begins. This book focuses on seasonal produce and the creativity of Bay Area chefs who work their magic with it.

Lisa Turner, *Meals That Heal, A Nutraceutical Approach to Diet and Health* (Rochester, Vt.: Healing Arts Press, 1996).

Turner's approach is not specifically focused on organic foods, but on fresh foods with nutritional and health-giving characteristics (such as antioxidants, lycopene) that we're just beginning to fully understand. There's plenty of science for those who want it, and the many wonderful recipes, easy to follow even for noncooks, are perfectly suited to the best organically grown ingredients.

Marcia and Jack Kelly, eds., *One Hundred Graces: Mealtime Blessings* (New York: Bell Tower, 1992).

No matter what kind of food you buy and eat, eat it with a spirit of gratitude and appreciation for those who helped grow it and bring it to the table. If you don't have a traditional family blessing, this small book offers mealtime blessings from cultures, religions, and communities around the world.

Periodicals

Saveur
www.saveurmag.com

Saveur is a beautiful magazine devoted to "authentic" cuisine—the best food and culinary traditions from around the globe. If you think there's no such thing as regional cooking anymore, read and savor *Saveur.*

Gourmet
www.gourmet.com

This venerable food magazine has a fresh look under new editor Ruth Reichl, and their Special Harvest Issue of September 2000 featured organic foods and issues on virtually every page. There's an on-line recipe database, too.

Natural Health
www.naturalhealthmagazine.com

Good coverage of all kinds of natural health issues and news, with good vegetarian recipes.

Food & Wine
www.foodandwine.com

A magazine for modern, trendy, and stylish gourmets, *Food & Wine* also has a Web site with an extensive recipe database. Though not strictly about organic foods, *Food & Wine* often profiles rising chefs with what might be called an organic sensibility—a commitment to fresh, flavorful, sustainable, and often local ingredients.

Martha Stewart Living
   www.marthastewart.com

Whether you love or hate her, Martha Stewart's print and broadcast enterprises often showcase local, organic, and artisan foods and products. Recently I heard Martha tell an interviewer that all her gardens were going to be certified organic in 2001, so maybe she'll begin to use her considerable clout to fully support organic agriculture.

Organizations and Educational Institutions

Chefs Collaborative/Oldways
   www.chefnet.com/cc2000

See All-Star Organizations for a complete listing for Chefs Collaborative, an organization not just for chefs, but for everyone who loves good food.

Culinary Institute of America/Culinary Institute at Greystone
   www.ciachef.edu

The Culinary Institute of America in Hyde Park, New York, and its California offshoot at Greystone in St. Helena in the Napa Valley offer continuing education and workshops for laypeople interested in learning some of the skills of professional chefs. At Greystone, the school is surrounded by organic gardens; at both schools, the administration has instituted a set of principles that embrace locally grown, organic, and sustainable agriculture and cuisine.

The American Center for Wine, Food and the Arts
   www.theamericancenter.org
   1700 Soscol Avenue, Suite 1
   Napa, CA 94559-1315
   (707) 257-3606

This center is scheduled to open in the fall of 2001 and plans to bring together chefs, home cooks, winemakers and wine lovers, artists, and more, "sharing their connections with food and wine as expressions of American culture." Set on 12 acres on the banks of the Napa River, the center will offer programs, classes, exhibitions, and demonstrations.

Slow Food
www.slowfood.com

Slow Food is an international movement dedicated to the pleasures of eating, to preserving local flavors and artisanal foods, and to celebrating gastronomic history and tradition. Visit the Web site to find connections in the United States or in countries you'd like to visit.

HEALTHY EATING, WHOLE FOODS, AND NUTRITION

These guidebooks to the world of health and diet, whole foods, and nutrition also include good recipes. Each is a very valuable resource to include on your kitchen bookshelf.

Andrew Weil, M.D., *Eating Well for Optimum Health: The Essential Guide to Food, Diet, and Nutrition* (New York: Knopf, 2000).

Dr. Andrew Weil's fame and popularity is so well deserved. He cuts right through health confusion and dogma to offer straightforward, specific information about the best medical and health solutions the world has to offer. This is his first book to focus exclusively on food and diet, with a suggested diet and eighty-five recipes designed for health, longevity, and flavor. Weil understands the importance of organic foods and has recommended them for many years. If you don't know whom to trust when it comes to diet and health books, start here. You're likely to find everything you need.

Margaret M. Wittenberg, *Good Food: The Complete Guide to Eating Well* (Santa Cruz, Calif.: Crossing Press, 1995).

This is an encyclopedic guide to facts, features, cooking guidelines, and health characteristics of foods, with a special focus on natural ingredients and concerns about additives and residues. A few well-chosen recipes round out this valuable resource.

Chris Kilham, *The Whole Food Bible: How to Select and Prepare Safe, Healthful Foods* (Rochester, Vt.: Inner Traditions, 1996).

The original edition of this useful resource on natural foods was published by Addison Wesley in 1991 under the auspices of Bread & Circus, a natural market chain in the Northeast now owned by Whole Foods Market. This updated edition contains, as did the first edition, excellent recipes by chef Catherine Conniff and others.

FOOD SAFETY

Responsible food safety practices are important no matter what kind of food you buy. In addition to Center for Science in the Public Interest (see All-Star Organizations), try these sites if you'd like to learn more about the best practices in food safety.

FoodSafety.gov: Gateway to Government Food Safety Information
www.foodsafety.gov

This is the Food and Drug Administration's Web site for consumers.

Centers for Disease Control Food Safety Initiative
www.cdc.gov/foodsafety

Links to CDC's information about food-borne diseases and pathogens, high-risk groups, outbreak investigations, educational and technical resources, and more.

ORGANIC COTTON

It's now possible to buy beautiful clothing, household goods, and personal care products made with organically grown cotton, helping to offset the serious environmental consequences of conventional cotton farming. The following resources can help you find specific products, whether baby clothing, sheets and towels, tree-free fine paper, or other goods.

Organic Trade Association's Organic Fiber Directory, 2d ed. (Greenfield, Mass.: Organic Trade Association, 2000).

This comprehensive directory lists companies throughout the supply chain that are part of the organic cotton movement. From growers to designers to wholesalers and retailers, this is an essential directory for anyone interested in organic cotton materials or finished goods. Contact Organic Trade Association for purchase information: (413) 775-7511, info@ota.com, www.ota.com.

Care What You Wear: A Consumer's Guide to Organic Cotton. (New York: Mothers & Others, 1999).

Published by Mothers & Others for a Livable Planet, a New York–based environmental advocacy and education organization, this is an excellent guide to the whys and wherefores of organic cotton, written for consumers and offering places to buy organic cotton clothing, household, and personal goods. Purchase for $5 from Mothers & Others, 40 West 20th Street, New York, NY 10011, (212) 242-0010, mothers@mothers.org, www.mothers.org.

Sustainable Cotton Project
www.sustainablecotton.org

A wonderful educational and informational Web site about organic cotton, complete with on-line directory and case studies of companies who've adopted organic cotton for all or part of their manufacturing process. Sustainable Cotton Project is funded by California and federal environmental protection agencies and a number of environmental foundations and nonprofits.

Fiber Ethics **magazine**
www.fiberethics.com

This new journal is dedicated to sustainable and environmentally responsible fabrics and textiles in the commercial, residential, and fashion markets. Their Web site includes an "eco directory" that will guide you to stores and companies selling organic cotton products and those made from other "eco-fabrics."

Patagonia, Inc.
www.patagonia.com

Among several large clothing/sporting gear companies that support organic cotton use, including Levi-Strauss and Nike, Patagonia deserves special mention for the degree of its commitment. In 1996, they began using only organic cotton wherever cotton was used in production. They've been generous in articulating both the challenges and rewards of this manufacturing conversion in order to help other companies do the same. Patagonia also publishes educational brochures for consumers on organic cotton.

CHILDREN AND PESTICIDES/ ENVIRONMENTAL HEALTH

The environmental health movement is growing rapidly, as science, medicine, and environmentalism join to yield a greater understanding of how pesticides and other toxins in the environment may affect human health. Some of these resources—again, just a few places to start—focus especially on the greater risk to children from environmental hazards. The reports created by and available through Environmental Working Group (see All-Star Organizations) are essential reading; here are additional resources.

Books

Sandra Steingraber, *Living Downstream: A Scientist's Personal Investigation of Cancer and the Environment* (New York: Vintage Books, 1997, 1998).

This is an extraordinary book, rigorous in its science and profound in its sensitivity and sense of poetry and beauty. Anyone whose life has been touched by cancer or who has concerns about environmental toxins should read this book.

John Wargo, *Our Children's Toxic Legacy: How Science and Law Fail to Protect Us from Pesticides* (New Haven: Yale University Press, 1996, 1998).

A serious book about pesticides, science, law, and the failures of all three to protect our children. While technically exact and comprehensive in its research, Wargo's writing is clear and accessible.

Theo Colborn, Dianne Dumanoski, and John Peterson Myers, *Our Stolen Future* (New York: Dutton, 1996).

This book, quite controversial when first published, calls itself a "scientific detective story." The book examines the so-called "endocrine disrupters"—chemicals in the environment that mimic hormones and may therefore play havoc with our health for many generations to come. It's a fascinating, sometimes frightening, but very worthwhile read.

Periodicals

Natural Home
www.naturalhomemagazine.com

If you'd like your home to be nontoxic, environmentally respon- sible, and both practical and beautiful throughout, this bimonthly publication, published by Interweave Press in Loveland, Colorado, will inspire you.

Organizations/Institutes

Preventing Harm.org
www.preventingharm.org

This Web site is a project of the Clean Water Fund. Through this site, you can download additional resources such as *In Harm's Way: Toxic Threats to Child Development,* a recent report by Greater Boston Physicians for Social Responsibility that, says the executive summary, "examines the contribution of toxic chemicals to neurodevelopmental, learning, and behavioral disabilities in chil- dren. . . . Toxic exposures deserve special scrutiny because they are *preventable* causes of harm."

Commonweal

www.commonweal.org

P.O. Box 316

Bolinas, CA 94924

(415) 868-0970

Commonweal is a nonprofit health and environmental research institute founded in 1976. Commonweal's work includes projects in cancer support, children's services and juvenile justice, and the Commonweal Health and Environment Program.

Silent Spring Institute

www.silentspring.org

29 Crafts Street

Newton, MA 02458

(617) 332-4288

E-mail: info@silentspring.org

The nonprofit Silent Spring Institute is named in honor of Rachel Carson's 1962 book, and its primary focus is researching links between environmental toxins and breast cancer. Through their Web site, you can access Silent Spring's Geographic Information System, a mapping database integrating health outcomes with historical environmental data, and other tools and publications.

Children's Environmental Health Network

www.cehn.org

110 Maryland Avenue NE, Suite 511

Washington, DC 20002

(202) 543-4033

E-mail: cehn@cehn.org

National project with an excellent on-line resource guide, indexed by keyword, geographical region, organizations, publications, and more.

American Environmental Health Foundation (AEHF)
www.aehf.com
1-800-428-aehf
E-mail: aehf@aehf.com

The American Environmental Health Foundation is a nonprofit organization founded in 1975 by William J. Rea, M.D., of the Dallas Environmental Health Center. Their Web site has a slew of research reports written for laypeople on safe schools, organic gardening, and more, as well as an on-line store with nontoxic products.

ORGANIC CERTIFIERS AND MATERIALS INFORMATION

If you'd like to know more about organic certification and specific materials allowed for use in organic farming, these are excellent resources. For information on the federal organic standard, see the listing for the USDA's National Organic Program.

Organic Materials Review Institute (OMRI)
www.omri.org
P.O. Box 11558
Eugene, OR 97440-3758
(541) 343-7600
E-mail: info@omri.org

OMRI is a nonprofit organization created to benefit the organic community and the general public. Its primary mission is to publish and disseminate generic and specific (brand name) lists of materials allowed and prohibited for use in the production, processing, and handling of organic food and fiber. OMRI also conducts scientific research and education on the use of materials by the organic industry.

National Organic Program (NOP) of the USDA
www.ams.usda.gov/nop

The National Organic Program is administered by the Agricultural Marketing Service of the United States Department of Agriculture. With the implementation of national standards finalized in 2000, products bearing the organic label in the United States must meet the certification regulations of the USDA. If you have questions about how the organic label is regulated and how organic certification operates under the federal umbrella, try the NOP Web site.

Oregon Tilth (Certifiers)
www.tilth.org
1860 Hawthorne Avenue NE, Suite 200
Salem, OR 97303
(503) 378-0690
E-mail: organic@tilth.org

Oregon Tilth helped pioneer organic certification in the West. Visit their Web site for research and education information, publications, newsletter, and more.

California Certified Organic Farmers (Certifiers)
www.ccof.org
1115 Mission Street
Santa Cruz, CA 95060
(831) 423-2263

Another pioneer in organic certification, CCOF publishes a quarterly journal, and its Web site will help you "find a farmer" or learn more about certification and the organic movement in California.

Northeast Organic Farmers' Association (NOFA)
www.nofa.org

NOFA is an affiliation of seven state chapters: Connecticut, Massachusetts, New Hampshire, New Jersey, New York, Rhode Island, and Vermont. They host a summer conference and other projects and are deeply involved in promoting organic foods and farmers in the Northeast. The central Web site has links to state chapters and information.

Independent Organic Certifiers Organization (IOIA)
www.ioia.net
P.O. Box 6
Broadus, MT 59317
(406) 436-2031
E-mail: ioia@ioia.net

IOIA is a nonprofit association of trained farm and processing inspectors. Founded in 1991, IOIA's mission is to provide the organic industry with trained and qualified inspectors to promote consistency in the inspection process that leads to certification. If you're interested in becoming an organic inspector, IOIA offers training programs; they'll also help you learn about how to get certified if you're a business, and their Web site has extensive links to certifying agents.

Demeter Association
www.demeter-usa.org
Britt Road
Aurora, NY 13026
(315) 364-5617

The Demeter Association certifies biodynamic farms, and its Web site has information about biodynamic farming practices and resources.

The Soil Association
www.soilassociation.org
Bristol House
40-56 Victoria Street
Bristol BS1 6BY
United Kingdom
(+44) (0) 117-929-0661
E-mail: info@soilassociation.org

The Soil Association is a membership-based nonprofit organization promoting organic food and farming in the United Kingdom. Their subsidiary Soil Association Certification Ltd. is the largest U.K. organic certifier. This is a great place to begin if you're looking for information on organic farming and foods in the United Kingdom and Europe.

BIODIVERSITY: BIRDS, BEES, FISH, AND MORE

Biological diversity is an important environmental principle at the very foundation of organic foods and farming. There are many resources devoted to biodiversity; just a few are listed here to get you started.

One sad aspect of agribusiness's wholesale pesticide-use practices, first illustrated poignantly by Rachel Carson in *Silent Spring,* is the decimation of populations of birds, bees, and other wildlife. Here, then, are also a few organizations that focus on specific issues of saving bees, birds, fish, and other species that are inadvertently targeted and seriously harmed by agricultural chemicals.

Books

Stephen L. Buchmann, Gary Paul Nabhan, and Paul Mirocha, *The Forgotten Pollinators* (Washington, D.C.: Island Press, 1997).

Bees and other pollinators are essential to a sustainable food supply, but many species are threatened. An entomologist, a bee researcher, and a crop ecologist look at the relationship between pollinators and plants. (Island Press is a nonprofit publisher of environmental books; visit their on-line book catalog at www.islandpress.com.)

Organizations

Smithsonian Migratory Bird Center
www.natzoo.si.edu/smbc/start.htm

Organic coffee and chocolate farming is especially important to populations of songbirds and to bird lovers. Who would want to live in a world without songbirds? To learn more about this important connection between sustainable growing in rain forest regions and the birds who sing in our backyards, visit the Smithsonian Migratory Bird Center's Web site. The site also has a list of bird-friendly and organic coffee companies.

American Bird Conservancy Pesticides and Birds Campaign
www.abcbirds.org/pesticideindex.htm
American Bird Conservancy
1250 24th Street NW, Suite 400
Washington, DC 20037
(202) 778-9666
E-mail: abc@abcbirds.org

The American Bird Conservancy (ABC) established this campaign in 1998 in response, they say, to "continuing pesticide-related bird kills throughout the Americas and a paucity of information and action on the issue." ABC estimates that millions of birds die annually from causes related to pesticide exposure.

Conservation International
www.conservation.org
2501 M Street NW, Suite 200
Washington, DC 20037
1-800-429-5660

This membership-based organization has a mission to "conserve Earth's living natural heritage, our global biodiversity, and to demonstrate that human societies are able to live harmoniously with nature." Theirs is a global focus, with lots of information on the planet's "hot spots" and projects that help promote responsible and ecological tourism.

Turning Point Project
www.turnpoint.org

See All-Star Organizations for complete listing. The global extinction crisis is one of Turning Point's key issues, and they offer a complete listing of related organizations and resources.

Center for Marine Conservation
www.cmc-ocean.org
1725 DeSales Street NW, Suite 600
Washington, DC 20036
(202) 429-5609
E-mail: cmc@dccmc.org

Oceans and sea life are at risk from pollution, including agricultural chemical runoff, and from coastal overdevelopment and overfishing. The Center for Marine Conservation will introduce you to key ocean issues.

**Chefs Collaborative/Environmental
Defense Sustainable Seafood Project**
   www.environmentaldefense.org/pubs/factsheets/s_fishchoices.html

   Both wild fishing and fish farming, or aquaculture, as widely practiced today, have grave environmental consequences. As yet, organic standards for fish have not been designed, but there is a growing awareness of the importance of choosing fish in the market that are not endangered, at risk, genetically engineered, or contributing to environmental harm through chemical practices involved in most aquaculture.
   Chefs Collaborative and Environmental Defense (see All-Star Organizations) offer educational information for chefs and consumers about which fish is best. Visit the above link to see the list of best-to-choose and best-to-avoid fishes, to download the full sustainable seafood report published jointly by the two orgnaizations, and to link to additional resources.

SMALL AND FAMILY FARMING

Learn about the farmers in your own region by shopping at the farmers market, joining a CSA, taking a farm tour if available, and buying local whenever you can. To increase your awareness of the larger farm crisis in this country and elsewhere and the consequences of an industrialized agriculture run amok, try these resources.
   I also recommend the essays and the books of Wendell Berry, David Mas Masumoto, Wes Jackson, and others who write about farming, a sense of place, and rural communities. See Recommended Reading: Community and Philosophy for specific listings.

Farm Aid
   (See complete listing in All-Star Organizations.)

American Farmland Trust (AFT)
www.farmland.org
1200 18th Street NW, Suite 800
Washington, DC 20036
(202) 331-7300
E-mail: info@farmland.org

American Farmland Trust was founded in 1980 to protect farmland. AFT's mission is to stop the loss of productive farmland and to promote farming practices that lead to a healthy environment. AFT's research arm is the Center for Agriculture in the Environment, based in DeKalb, Illinois. The center's Web site is www.farmlandinfo.org.

Community Alliance with Family Farmers (CAFF)
www.caff.org
P.O. Box 363
Davis, CA 95617
(530) 756-8518

CAFF is a nonprofit membership organization whose mission is to build a movement of rural and urban people who foster family-scale agriculture. CAFF publishes the annual *National Organic Directory* and, on its Web site, offers guides to California farmers markets and CSA farms.

National Family Farm Coalition (NFFC)
www.nffc.net
110 Maryland Avenue NE, Suite 307
Washington, DC 20002
E-mail: nffc@nffc.net

NFFC, founded in 1986, links grassroots organizations working on family farm issues in thirty-three states.

New England Small Farm Institute
www.smallfarm.org
275 Jackson Street
Belchertown, MA 01007
(413) 323-4531
E-mail: info@smallfarm.org

The New England Small Farm Institute is a private nonprofit
organization supporting beginning farmers and sustainable small-
scale agriculture in New England. Through the Web site, link to
their Small Farm Library, Northeast Workers on Organic Farms
(an apprenticeship network), business training/entrepreneurship
links, and more.

Turning Point Project
www.turnpoint.org

See All-Star Organizations for complete listing. Industrial agriculture and its consequences is one of Turning Point's key
issues, and they offer an excellent guide to related organizations
and resources.

Barn Again!
www.agriculture.com/ba/ba!home.html
National Trust for Historic Preservation
Barn Again! Program
910 16th Street, Suite 1100
Denver, CO 80202

If you love old barns, or own one and would like to restore it,
don't miss the chance to learn more about this project. Barn Again!
is a national program to preserve historic farm buildings, sponsored
by the National Trust for Historic Preservation and *Successful Farming* magazine. You'll find publications, awards, advice on barn
restoration, and a treasure trove of resources for barn lovers.

FARMERS MARKETS, COMMUNITY-SUPPORTED AGRICULTURE, AND FOOD CO-OPS

Farmers markets, community-supported agriculture, and food co-ops offer consumers the opportunity to buy directly from farmers and to have "alternative access" outside of supermarket chains. Fortunately, these grassroots and local enterprises are now linked through extensive on-line databases. Or call your local newspaper's food editor or agriculture reporter for farmers markets and CSA farms in your area.

USDA Farmers Markets List
www.ams.usda.gov/farmersmarkets/map.htm

The Agricultural Marketing Service of the United States Department of Agriculture maintains a database of farmers markets throughout the country. They also operate a Farmers Market Hotline at 1-800-384-8704.

Ask Dr. Weil Farmers Market Finder
www.eatingwell.net/market_finder.shtml

Search a national database of three thousand farmers markets by state and city. The home page, www.eatingwell.net, takes you to Ask Dr. Weil's healthy eating programs.

Directory of Public Farmers Market Web Sites
www.marketfarm.homestead.com/marketsites~ns4.html

Visit market Web sites for seasonal guides, recipes, links to farmers, and more.

Biodynamic Farming and Gardening Association (BDA)
www.biodynamics.com
P.O. Box 29135
San Francisco, CA 94129-0135

1-888-516-7797
E-mail: biodynamic@aol.com

BDA is a nonprofit organization that fosters, guides, and safe-guards the biodynamic method of agriculture, begun by Rudolf Steiner in 1924. The Web site hosts a mirror site of USDA's CSA farms database and also has its own database of community-supported agriculture farms, specifying which are certified organic or biodynamic.

Robyn Van En Center/CSA Resources in the Northeast
www.csacenter.org
Wilson College Center for Sustainable Living
1015 Philadelphia Avenue
Chambersburg, PA 17201
(717) 261-2880
E-mail: info@csacenter.org

The Robyn Van En Center supports the CSA movement with information and education. Click through their site to a resource center and library, a database of CSA farms in the United States, and mail-order publications.

Community Supported Agriculture of North America at University of Massachusetts Extension
www.umass.edu/umext/csa/

Good educational information about CSA farms and a very good resource list.

Directory of Food Co-ops and Other Co-op Resources
www.columbia.edu/~jw157/food.coop.html

This excellent site is maintained by an individual, not an organization, but has a state-by-state database, listings of Web food co-ops, on-line vendors for those who'd like to start or expand a co-op, resources, and more.

National Cooperative Business Association (NCBA)
www.cooperative.org
1401 New York Avenue NW, Suite 1100
Washington, DC 20005
(202) 638-6222
E-mail: ncba@ncba.org

NCBA is a resource guide to information about cooperative businesses of all kinds, including food co-ops. Whether you want to find a co-op, start one, or learn more about their principles, this is an excellent starting point.

ORGANIC FARMING RESEARCH, EDUCATION, AND INTERNSHIPS

These organizations conduct or fund organic farming research, place interns, or offer education and information for those with a serious interest in organic farming. Look also for master gardener and continuing education classes at local universities with agriculture programs; more and more of them are teaching classes that use and reflect organic methods and principles.

Organic Farming Research Foundation (OFRF)
www.ofrf.org

See complete listing in All-Star Organizations. Note OFRF's publications: Every two years, they publish the results of a comprehensive survey of organic farmers in the United States. And in 1998, OFRF published *Searching for the "O-Word,"* by Mark Lipson, an illuminating analysis of current funding (and lack thereof) for organic projects. OFRF also funds on-farm research into organic methods.

The Rodale Institute
www.rodaleinstitute.org
Rodale Institute Experimental Farm
611 Siegfriedale Road
Kutztown, PA 19530
(610) 683-1400
E-mail: info@rodaleinst.org

The Rodale Institute is descended from the original foundation created by J. I. Rodale in 1947. Today, the Rodale Institute conducts research on its experimental farm with a focus on soil health, food quality, food systems education, composting, and community development. The institute also conducts outreach projects domestically and internationally.

Willing Workers on Organic Farms (WWOOF)
www.wwoof.org

Think you might like to try your hand at organic farming—maybe in New Zealand, Italy, or some other exotic locale? WWOOF is an international nonprofit organization that places volunteers on organic farms around the world.

Northeast Workers on Organic Farms (NEWOOF)
www.smallfarm.org/newoof/newoof.html

NEWOOF, sponsored by the New England Small Farm Institute, publishes a list of farms seeking apprentices in this country, primarily in the Northeast.

Sustainable Agriculture Network (SAN) and
Sustainable Agriculture Research and Education Program (SARE)
www.sare.org

SAN is the communications and outreach arm of the SARE program, a USDA-funded initiative that sponsors grants for sustainable agriculture research and education nationwide. SARE's research and education grants reach universities and nonprofit organizations in an interdisciplinary approach, they say.

Henry A. Wallace Center for Agricultural &
Environmental Policy at Winrock International
www.hawiaa.org

The Wallace Center publishes *Alternative Agriculture News* and *American Journal of Alternative Agriculture.* Among its projects are the Agriculture Policy Project, which seeks to "engage people at the local, regional, and national levels in the development of long-term, proactive policies for sustainable food and agriculture systems."

Alternative Farming Systems Information Center (AFSIC)
www.nal.usda.gov/afsic
10301 Baltimore Avenue, Room 304
Beltsville, MD 20705-2351
(301) 504-6559
E-mail: afsic@nal.usda.gov

The Information Center is part of the USDA's National Agricultural Library. Links take you to extensive information on sustainable agriculture and community-supported agriculture, including a guide to sustainable agriculture university education and training programs.

Jane Potter Gates and volunteer staff, comp., *Educational and Training Opportunities in Sustainable Agriculture*, 12th ed. (Washington, D.C.: National Agricultural Library, 2000). Available at www.nal.usda.gov/afsic/AFSIC_pubs/edtr12.htm.

Appropriate Technology Transfer for Rural Areas (ATTRA)
www.attra.org
P.O. Box 3657
Fayetteville, AR 72702
1-800-346-9140

ATTRA is a national sustainable farming information center operated by the private nonprofit National Center for Appropriate Technology. The ATTRA Web site has excellent resource lists of organizations and publications; non-GMO, nonhybrid, and heirloom seed suppliers; sustainable agriculture curricula for grades K–12; and a complete guide to sustainable farming internships and apprenticeships.

UCSC Farm & Garden Apprenticeship Program
http://zzyx.ucsc.edu/casfs

Center for Agroecology & Sustainable Food Systems (CASFS)
University of California
1156 High Street
Santa Cruz, CA 95064
(408) 459-4140

Both of the above programs, operating since 1967, are a six-month training ground in organic farming that has graduated more than seven hundred farmers, gardeners, and leaders in sustainable agriculture and community. Apprentices live and work on the 25-acre farm and 2-acre garden at the base of the beautiful University of California at Santa Cruz campus. Apprentices also help run a farmers market stand and a community-supported agriculture project. Scholarship funds are available to qualified applicants.

The Land Institute
www.landinstitute.org
2440 East Water Well Road
Salina, KS 67401
(785) 823-5376
E-mail: theland@landinstitute.org

The Land Institute is a nonprofit environmental education and research organization focused on connections between land, people, and community. With a focus on "natural systems agriculture," the Land Institute offers intensive weekend courses and seasonal research positions for undergraduates as well as research grants and career counseling for graduate students. Environmentalist and author Wes Jackson founded and is the leader of the institute.

Ecological Farming Conference
www.eco-farm.org
Ecological Farming Association
406 Main Street, Suite 313
Watsonville, CA 95076

This annual conference, held at the beautiful Asilomar conference center on the Pacific coast outside Monterey, California, attracts organic advocates of all kinds as well as farmers.

GENETIC ENGINEERING IN FOOD AND AGRICULTURE

These resources will help you learn more about genetic modification and engineering in food and agriculture (also called transgenic technologies because genes are transferred across species). GMOs are also a current events story, however, so keep up with the news in local and international print and broadcast news sources; in fact, some of the best writing about genetically modified foods is being published in periodicals right now (see Bibliography for some of these). A word of caution: There's a lot of "spin" out there about genetically modified foods on both sides of the battle. However, the precautionary principle that technologies ought to be proved safe, not just "not proved dangerous," can be a helpful guideline.

Books

Jane Rissler and Margaret Mellon, *The Ecological Risks of Engineered Crops* (Cambridge, Mass.: MIT Press, 1996).

A serious work of science evaluating the risks and potential risk scenarios of transgenic technologies in agriculture.

Marc Lappe and Britt Bailey, *Against the Grain: Biotechnology and the Corporate Takeover of Your Food* (Monroe, Maine: Common Courage Press, 1998).

Argues against the argument that biotechnology is "necessary to feed the world."

Laura Ticciati and Robin Ticciati, *Genetically Engineered Foods: Are They Safe? You Decide* (Los Angeles: Keats, 1998).

Laura Ticciati is the director of Mothers for Natural Law, a nonprofit organization working to educate consumers about biotechnology.

Organizations

Citizens for Health
www.citizens.org

Citizens for Health is a nonprofit, grassroots, advocacy organization for natural health consumers. Their "Keep Nature Natural" campaign was launched to help educate consumers about genetic modification and to work with legislators to try to fight unlabeled, uncontained GMOs in foods and agriculture.

Organic Consumers Association
www.purefood.org

The Organic Consumers Association works for organic choices and against genetic engineering, irradiation, hormones, and other food additives and processes.

Turning Point Project
www.turnpoint.org

See All-Star Organizations for complete listing. Genetic engineering is one of Turning Point's key issues, and they offer a guide to related organizations and resources.

INFORMATION FOR TEACHERS AND KIDS

Let's Get Growing! Company Catalog
www.letsgetgrowing.com
1900 Commercial Way
Santa Cruz, CA 95065
1-800-408-1868

Let's Get Growing is a wonderful catalog of environmental science and nature supplies. Much of it is designed for the classroom, with gardening and habitat kits, teaching tools, garden supplies, and science discovery materials, but would also be fun for home-schoolers or just biologically curious children. If you'd like to help your child's school start an organic garden, you'll find the perfect tools here for growing and learning.

The Edible Schoolyard
www.edibleschoolyard.org

The Edible Schoolyard is a pilot program for schoolyard gardening at the Martin Luther King Jr. Middle School in Berkeley, California, started by chef Alice Waters. Today the garden is thriving and a kitchen classroom has been constructed. Waters is taking her program to other schools and hopes to see it become a nationwide movement. Visit the Web site for information about the project and how it works in practice.

Resource List: Sustainable Agriculture Curricula, Grades K–12
www.attra.org/attra-rl/k12.html

This list is compiled by Katherine Adam, a program specialist at Appropriate Technology Transfer for Rural Areas (ATTRA). The list is designed for use by teachers.

ORGANIC GARDENING: ORGANIC, NATIVE, AND HEIRLOOM SEEDS

Although most of this book talks about organic foods in the marketplace, home gardening is one of the very best ways to reconnect to where food comes from. Even if you just use containers or window boxes, it's a safe and very popular way to spend time outdoors, it's a great way for kids to learn about food and biology, and it rewards you with fresh foods, herbs, flowers, and even medicinal plants grown without chemicals.

There's also a whole world of community gardening, urban gardening, schoolyard gardens, and "therapeutic" gardens such as prison gardens, homeless gardens, and gardens designed for the disabled. There's little doubt that an organic garden on almost any scale can add to our sense of health, purpose, community, and security.

It always makes sense to start with local resources when it comes to seeds and gardening materials to find what best suits your local climate. That said, there are vast resources for gardeners in print, on the Internet, and through personal exchanges. This list is by no means comprehensive, but offers a few places to begin learning more about gardening with organic methods and, if you like, exploring the world of heirloom and native seeds.

Books

Howard-Yana Shapiro, Ph.D., and John Harrison, *Gardening for the Future of the Earth* (New York: Bantam Books, 2000).

Shapiro is the founder of Seeds of Change (see page 189), and this beautiful book will inspire you to embrace the principles of organic gardening and also to explore the world of heirloom plant varieties.

Maria Rodale, *Maria Rodale's Organic Gardening* (Emmaus, Pa.: Rodale Press, 1998).

Rodale Press publishes *Organic Gardening* magazine and many books on various aspects of organic gardening. They are part of the greater Rodale family, which includes the Rodale Institute, a center that conducts important research on soil fertility and farming. Maria Rodale's book is coffee-table-worthy—a stunning celebration of the beauty of the garden.

Eliot Coleman, *The New Organic Grower: A Master's Manual of Tools and Techniques for the Home and Market Gardener.* (White River Junction, Vt.: Chelsea Green, 1989, 1995).

Coleman's book is a classic, comprehensive guide for serious gardeners and small-market farmers. (Visit Chelsea Green's Web site at www.chelseagreen.com for more books on organic gardening and small farming and many other aspects of sustainable living.)

Shepherd Ogden, *Straight-Ahead Organic* (White River Junction, Vt.: Chelsea Green, 1992, 1999).

Solid, knowledgeable, and straightforward gardening advice from the cofounder of Cook's Garden catalog and seed supplier.

Suzanne Ashworth and David Cavagnaro, *Seed to Seed* (Decorah, Iowa: Seed Savers Publications, 1995).

This is a bible of heirloom gardening, published by the Seed Savers Exchange in Decorah, Iowa, which maintains many thousands of rare vegetable varieties at its farm. If you're interested in biodiversity, finding nonhybrid seeds, and heirloom gardening, this is a wonderful resource.

William Woys Weaver, *Heirloom Vegetable Gardening: A Master Gardener's Guide to Planting, Seed Saving, and Cultural History* (New York: Holt, 1999).

A wonderful resource full of food history, botanical lore, and gardening, as well as recipes.

Joe Smillie and Grace Gershuny, *The Soul of Soil: A Soil-Building Guide for Master Gardeners and Farmers,* 4th ed. (White River Junction, Vt.: Chelsea Green, 1999).

A gardener's guide to the intricate and complex world of the soil and how to enrich it naturally for organic gardening and farming success.

Periodicals

Rodale's Organic Gardening
www.organicgardening.com

Rodale's venerable magazine is still full of valuable information after decades of being the voice of organic gardeners in this country.

Taunton's Kitchen Gardener
www.taunton.com/kg/

This magazine is inspiring, taking the concept of "kitchen gardening" to new heights. While *KG* doesn't focus exclusively on organic methods, there is an appreciation for safe methods and fresh, wonderful produce.

Organizations

American Community Gardening Association (ACGA)
www.communitygarden.org
100 North 20th Street, 5th Floor
Philadelphia, PA 19103-1495
(215) 988-8785
E-mail: smccabe@pennhort.org

Membership-based national nonprofit organization of both professionals and volunteers involved in urban and rural community gardening.

Eastern Native Seed Conservancy
http://gemini.berkshire.net/ensc/index.html
222 Main Street
P.O. Box 451
Great Barrington, MA 01230
(413) 229-8316
E-mail: NatSeeds@aol.com

The Conservancy is a small nonprofit organization dedicated to preserving local food resources. Projects include the CRESS Heirloom Seed Conservation Project, creating a regional living seed bank, and the Native Seeds Project, which focuses on preserving the oldest domesticated plants from the Northeast region.

Web Sites

Horticulture Resource List: Suppliers of Organic, Non-GE [non–genetically engineered], or Heirloom [open-pollinated] Seed
www.attra.org/attra-pub/altseed.html

This list is compiled by Katherine Adam and published by Appropriate Technology Transfer for Rural Areas (ATTRA). Indexed by region, the list includes retail, wholesale, and cooperative sources for seeds, making it useful for both home gardeners and farmers.

The Heirloom Gardening Page
www.interl.net/~waylin47/

Created and maintained by organic farmer Matt Green, a lover of heirloom gardening and a true believer in self-sufficiency, this site has a lengthy list of seed companies complete with personal anecdotes and recommendations, along with a wealth of other information. From here, you can locate a number of Web sites and contact information for print catalogs.

Catalogs

Seeds of Change

www.seedsofchange.com

Seeds of Change is a seed company and much more. Their stunning seed catalog, offering organic, heirloom, rare, and native seeds as well as tools, gifts, and books, is a pleasure even for nongardeners. Their organic salsas and other foods (now owned by Mars) are available in natural foods stores nationwide. And their Web site is highly educational and informative.

The Cook's Garden

www.cooksgarden.com

Founded by Shepherd and Ellen Ogden, Cook's Garden is committed to organic methods and selling seeds free of chemical treatments and genetic modification, though they do sell some hybrid seeds that meet their criteria.

Southern Exposure Seed Exchange

www.southernexposure.com

Their motto is "Saving the Past for the Future." They provide on-line descriptions and a print catalog of more than 550 varieties of open-pollinated, heirloom, and traditional vegetables.

Victory Seeds
www.victoryseeds.com

In addition to seeds for vegetables, herbs, and flowers, Victory Seeds has gifts, including plant and flower boxes and birdhouses and feeders. They're based in Oregon.

Notes

INTRODUCTION

1. The Organic Trade Association, in its "Business Facts" fact sheet available at www.ota.com, cites *Natural Foods Merchandiser,* a trade magazine, as measuring organic industry growth at 20 percent or greater for the past nine years. Other estimates of growth are in the 15 percent range. This is due, in part, to the fast-growing nature of a relatively new industry.

2. In organic circles, the concept of the "organic Twinkie" is often held up as a warning, but sometimes it does seem that that is the direction we're headed. I believe that credit for the concept of the "organic Twinkie" goes to Joan Dye Gussow, Ed.D., a professor emeritus of nutrition and education at Teachers College of Columbia University. Gussow has campaigned passionately against allowing organic foods to become a mirror of the conventional food system, with its highly processed, nutritionally empty products.

CHAPTER ONE

1. The Rodale Institute, "Research at the Rodale Institute Challenges Toughest Critics of Organics." Press release, 15 March 2000. Although research overall remains limited, the Rodale Institute recently released results of a nineteen-year Farming Systems Trial, concluding that "organic methods are as efficient, economical, and financially competitive as conventional methods, as well as better for the soil and the environment."

2. This is a somewhat condensed version. The full definition, passed by the National Organic Standards Board at its April 1995 meeting (available at

www.ota.com) also includes the following: "*Organic* is a labeling term that denotes products produced under the authority of the Organic Foods Production Act. . . . Organic agriculture practices cannot ensure that products are completely free of residues; however, methods are used to minimize pollution from air, soil, and water. Organic food handlers, processors, and retailers adhere to standards that maintain the integrity of organic agricultural products."

3. John Wargo, *Our Children's Toxic Legacy* (New Haven, Conn.: Yale University Press, 1998), 4, referencing A. Aspelin, "Pesticide Industry Sales and Usage: 1992 and 1993 Market Estimates" (Washington, D.C.: EPA, June 1994).

4. Ibid., 162–171. The most notorious of these chemicals is probably DDT, still manufactured in the United States though banned for use in this country; in March 2000, the Associated Press reported that negotiators from more than one hundred countries were discussing a treaty to ban DDT globally.

5. Natural Resources Defense Council, "Eating What Comes Naturally." Available at http://www.nrdc.org/health/farming/forg101.asp. Revised 15 April 2000. Retrieved 25 October 2000. "One-third of our nation's topsoil has eroded due to modern industrialized farming practices."

6. John Wargo, *Our Children's Toxic Legacy* (New Haven, Conn.: Yale University Press, 1998), 151.

7. Center for Marine Conservation, "The Ocean: How You Can Help." 1998. Available at www.cmc-ocean.org/3_pt/34_howyou.php3. "Buy organic, locally grown produce when you can. Agricultural runoff introduces thousands of pounds of fertilizers and pesticides into the ocean every year."

8. Gary Kline, "Biodiversity and Development." *Journal of Third World Studies* 15, no. 1 (April 1998): 125. "Industrial monoculture has deleterious consequences for the land and environment."

9. Erica Walz, *Final Results of the Third Biennial National Organic Farmers' Survey* (Santa Cruz, Calif.: Organic Farming Research Foundation, 1999). Farmers surveyed farmed an average of 140 acres organically; most had plans to increase acreage.

10. Richard Wiles et al., "Overexposed: Organophosphate Insecticides in Children's Food." Washington, D.C.: Environmental Working Group/The Tides Center, 1998.

11. John Wargo, *Our Children's Toxic Legacy* (New Haven, Conn.: Yale University Press, 1998), 172–218.

CHAPTER TWO

1. For specific information on synthetic substances allowed in organic production, the reader is referred to the Web site of the National Organic Program (www.ams.usda.gov/nop) or contact the organizations listed under Organic Certifiers and Materials Information in Resources.

2. Jennifer D. Mitchell, "Nowhere to Hide: The Global Spread of High-Risk Synthetic Chemicals." *World Watch* 10, no. 2 (March/April 1997): 26.

3. Marianne Cleemann, "Persistent Organic Pollutants (POPs) in the Arctic Fauna." 1997. Available at www.dsf.gl/Inussuk/4foodtab/kap10.html.

4. The National Organic Standards Board may also recommend to the USDA standards for an organic label for fish. Standards may soon exist for wool fiber as well as cotton.

5. Organic Trade Association, "Manure Use and Agricultural Practices" and "Fact Sheet on *E. coli.*" 2000. Available at www.ota.com.

6. See food safety resources in Resources.

7. Erica Walz, *Final Results of the Third Biennial National Organic Farmers' Survey* (Santa Cruz, Calif.: Organic Farming Research Foundation, 1999).

8. Mary Jane Incorvia Mattina, William Iannucci-Berger, and Laure Dykas, "Chlordane Uptake and Its Translocation in Food Crops." *Journal of Agricultural and Food Chemistry* 48, no. 5 (15 May 2000). Available at http://pubs.acs.org/hotartcl/jafcau/2000/jf990566a_rev.html.

9. Mark Lipson, *Searching for the "O-Word"* (Santa Cruz, Calif.: Organic Farming Research Foundation, 1997).

10. The Rodale Institute, "Research at the Rodale Institute Challenges Toughest Critics of Organic." Press release, 15 March 2000.

CHAPTER THREE

1. This list has been widely used, and there are many variations in print and on the Internet. All share the right spirit of honoring the many positive reasons to support organic farming. I acknowledge the original author with respect and thanks.

CHAPTER FOUR

1. Elena Wilken, "Assault of the Earth," *World Watch* 8, no. 2 (March/April 1995): 20. Agriculture contributes to soil erosion and requires deliberate conservation techniques to offset it. But conventional agriculture contributes to a rate of topsoil erosion that, Wilken says, "as we try to grow more and more food—by cultivating marginal cropland, by intensifying production, by using more powerful technologies—our soils deteriorate."

2. Gary Kline, "Biodiversity and Development." *Journal of Third World Studies* 15, no. 1 (April 1998): 125.

3. Ibid., quoting Edward Osborne Wilson, ed., *Biodiversity* (Washington, D.C.: National Academy Press, 1989).

4. Ibid.

5. David E. Ervin et al., "Agriculture and Environment: A New Strategic Vision." *Environment* 40, no. 6 (July/August 1998).

6. Stefano Pagiola et al., "Mainstreaming Biodiversity in Agricultural Development." *Finance & Development* 35, no. 1 (March 1998): 38.

7. Keith Schneider, "In an Old Orchard, Tastes the Supermarket Forgot." *New York Times,* Science, 2 June 1998.

8. Organic Trade Association, "Manure Use and Agricultural Practices" and "Fact Sheet on *E. coli.*" 2000. Available at www.ota.com.

9. Elaine Lipson, "A Delicious Inheritance." *Natural Foods Merchandiser* 21, no. 3 (March 2000): 102. I interviewed Alan Kapuler for this story.

10. Seeds of Change, "Glossary of Terms." Available at http://store.yahoo.com/seedsofchange/glossary.html. Revised 15 January 2000.

11. Elaine Lipson, "A Delicious Inheritance." *Natural Foods Merchandiser* 21, no. 3 (March 2000): 102. Dr. Kapuler's quotes come from this story.

CHAPTER FIVE

1. Theo Colborn et al., *Our Stolen Future* (New York: Dutton, 1996). Colborn's book is perhaps the best-known analysis of these chemicals.

2. John Wargo, *Our Children's Toxic Legacy* (New Haven, Conn.: Yale University Press, 1998), 38.

3. Ibid., 42.

4. Rachel Carson, *Silent Spring* (New York: Houghton Mifflin, 1962), xv. From the introduction by Vice President Al Gore (1994).

5. Ibid., xxi.

6. Wargo, *Our Children's Toxic Legacy* (New Haven, Conn: Yale University Press, 1998), 51.

7. Ibid., 5.

8. Biodynamic Farming and Gardening Association. Available at www. biodynamics.com.

9. Elaine Lipson, "A Brief History of the National Organic Standards." *California Certified Organic Farmers' Newsletter* 15, no. 1 (Spring 1998): 4–11.

10. Apple growers brought suit against both the Natural Resources Defense Council and *60 Minutes,* but the suit was dismissed by the Ninth Circuit Court of Appeals on 2 October 1995. Ironically, this was the same day the O. J. Simpson verdict was announced, so few people heard the news that the reports on Alar had been vindicated. For more, see Charles Fulwood, "Right from the Start: The Case Against Alar," available at www.nrdc.org.

CHAPTER SIX

1. USDA release No. 0426.00, "Secretary Glickman's remarks at NOP Press Conference 20 December 2000." Available at www.ams.usda.gov/nop/glickremarks. htm.

2. Ibid.

3. The final rule for national organic standards was published in the Federal Register on 21 December 2000. It is also available in full on-line at www.ams. usda.gov/nop, along with accessible fact sheets that outline the highlights of the rule.

CHAPTER SEVEN

1. A number of longtime organic industry participants have mentioned this to me anecdotally.

2. Mark Lipson, "The First 'Eco-label': Lessons from the Organic Experience." Paper submitted to the proceedings of "Eco Labeling for California Winegrapes" workshop, Sacramento, California, February 1998.

3. It bears repeating: The full definition of organic, as recommended by the National Organic Standards Board, says that "Organic agriculture practices cannot ensure that products are completely free of residues; however, methods are used to minimize pollution from air, soil, and water" (www.ota.com// abouto.htm).

4. John Casey, "Not Just Ugly: Urban Grime May Contain Toxic Chemicals." *CBS Healthwatch,* 31 July 2000. Retrieved 11 August 2000. Available at http:// healthwatch.medscape.com/medscape/p/gcommunity/hnews.asp?/recid=22051.

5. The USDA's Food Safety and Inspection Service offers a Web page of meat and poultry labeling terms at www.fsis.usda.gov/oa/pubs/lablterm.htm. Revised February 1999. Retrieved 26 November 2000. The full definition of "free-range or free-roaming" is as follows: "Producers must demonstrate to the Agency that the poultry has been allowed access to the outside."

6. Look for certified biodynamic produce certified by the Demeter Association. See Resources to connect with both the Biodynamic Farming and Gardening Association and Demeter.

7. Kagan Owens and Jay Feldman, "The Schooling of State Pesticide Laws." *Pesticides and You* 18, no. 3 (1998): 20. "Thirteen states define, recommend, or require IPM in their state pesticide statutes or regulations." See article for state-by-state IPM regulations as they apply to schools.

CHAPTER EIGHT

1. These statistics come from the Farm Aid Web site at www.farmaid.org, where they are cited from the 1997 Census of Agriculture and the USDA Economic Research Service. Similar numbers are cited in Wendell Berry's essay "Conserving Communities," from *Another Turn of the Crank* (Washington, D.C.: Counterpoint, 1995).

2. Steven Gorelick, "Facing the Farm Crisis." *The Ecologist* 30, no. 4 (June 2000): 28–31.

3. Environmental Working Group's Hogwatch Web site, at www.hogwatch.org, graphically illustrates what industrial hog farming has done in North Carolina.

4. See Resources for information on the Turning Point Project, which has industrial agriculture as a key focus and an excellent brochure with additional resources (www.turnpoint.org).

5. Again, see www.turnpoint.org and full listing in Resources.

6. Wes Jackson, *Becoming Native to This Place* (Washington, D.C.: Counterpoint, 1994, 1996).

7. Erica Walz, *Final Results of the Third Biennial National Organic Farmers' Survey* (Santa Cruz, Calif.: Organic Farming Research Foundation, 1999), 46. Laura Tourte is quoted in the survey.

8. The books of Victor Davis Hanson are eloquent, if challenging, explorations of our myths and beliefs about farmers. See Bibliography.

CHAPTER NINE

1. Paul Kingsnorth, "Bovine Growth Hormones." *The Ecologist* 28, no. 5 (October 1998).

2. See CSPI listing in Resources and visit www.cspi-net.com.

3. Organic Valley Cooperative released a press release concerning their lawsuit. See "rBGH Lawsuit Settlement" at http://www.organicvalley.com/PR-rbgh.htm. Retrieved 18 March 2000.

4. Animal Welfare Institute, "rBGH Ruled Unsafe for Canadian and European People and Cows." *Animal Welfare Institute Quarterly* 48, no. 2 (Spring 1999). Available at www.animalwelfare.com/farm/rbgh-s99.htm.

5. USDA News Release, "Organic Labeling Claim Allowed on Meat and Poultry Products," 14 January 1999.

6. John Wargo, *Our Children's Toxic Legacy* (New Haven, Conn.: Yale University Press, 1998), 133. "Further, nearly 53 percent of all herbicides applied in 1991 were used on only three crops: corn, soybeans, and cotton."

7. Consumers Union, "Seeds of Change." *Consumer Reports* (September 1999): 41. Estimates that nearly half of all cotton crops are genetically engineered.

8. Shelley A. Hearne, *Harvest of Unknowns: Pesticide Contamination in Imported Foods* (New York: Natural Resources Defense Council, 1984), 14–18.

9. Natural Resources Defense Council, "Coffee, Conservation, and Commerce in the Western Hemisphere." New York: Natural Resources Defense Council and Smithsonian Migratory Bird Center, 1996.

10. Smithsonian Migratory Bird Center, "Why Migratory Birds Are Crazy for Coffee." Available at http://natzoo.si.edu/smbc/fxshts/fxsht1a.htm. SMBC's site also has an on-line list of coffee companies selling organic or coffee considered "bird-friendly" by SMBC.

CHAPTER TEN

1. See Resources for links to food co-op databases and the National Cooperative Business Association, which can help you start a co-op of any kind.

2. See www.iceland.co.uk for the company's policy on organic foods.

3. The Foreign Agricultural Service of the USDA tracks the growth of the organic market in many countries, especially as it pertains to U.S. exporters. The International Federation of Organic Agriculture Movements (IFOAM, at www.ifoam.org) has extensive information about organics around the world. See also The Soil Association's briefing papers at www.soilassociation.org.

4. Center for Integrated Agricultural Systems, "Research Brief #21: Community Supported Agriculture: Growing Food and Community." Available at www.wisc.edu/cias/pubs/briefs/021.html. Revised 10 November 2000. Retrieved 27 November 2000.

5. Jack P. Cooley and Daniel A. Lass, "What's Your Share Worth? Some Comparisons of CSA Share Cost Versus Retail Produce Value." Available at http://klaatu.oit.umass.edu/resec/fac+staff/csa2.html. Retrieved 26 August 2000.

6. Visit Hedgerow Farm's Web site at http://www.naropa.edu/hedgerow/.

CHAPTER ELEVEN

1. For a very good report on the current issues and available research, see Steve Diver, *Nutritional Quality of Organically Grown Food* (Fayetteville, Ark.: Appropriate Technology Transfer for Rural Areas, September 2000). Available at http://ncatark.uark.edu/~steved/food-quality.html. Retrieved 26 November 2000.

2. Joan Dye Gussow, "But Is It More Nutritious?" *Eating Well* (May/June 1997): 38.

CHAPTER TWELVE

1. Consumers Union, "Seeds of Change." *Consumer Reports* (September 1999): 45.

2. See the USDA's standards at www.ams.usda.gov/nop.

3. Matthew Feldmann et al., "Why So Much Controversy Over Genetically Modified Organisms? Answers to 10 Frequently Asked Questions About GMOs." International Maize and Wheat Improvement Center, 7 February 2000. Available at http://www.cimmyt.mx/research/abc/10-faqaboutgmos/htm/10-faqaboutgmos.htm.

4. Consumers Union, "Seeds of Change." *Consumer Reports* (September 1999).

5. The Union of Concerned Scientists' Web site lists genetically engineered crops allowed in the U.S. food supply. Available at http://www.ucsusa.org/agriculture/gen.market.html. Retrieved 28 June 2000.

6. Midwest Sustainable Agriculture Working Group, "Midwest Sustainable Agriculture Working Group Position Paper on Genetic Engineering," 24 February 2000. Available at http://www.cfra.org/MSAWG-GE.htm. Retrieved 3 March 2000.

7. Miguel A. Altieri and Peter Rosset, *Ten Reasons Why Biotechnology Will Not Ensure Food Security, Protect the Environment and Reduce Poverty in the Developing World* (Oakland, Calif.: Food First/Institute for Food and Development Policy, October 1999).

8. Jane Rissler and Margaret Mellon, *The Ecological Risk of Engineered Crops* (Cambridge, Mass.: MIT Press, 1996), offers a complete scientific analysis of the environmental risks of genetic engineering.

9. J. Madeleine Nash, "Grains of Hope," *Time* 156, no. 5 (31 July 2000): 45. The "Weighing the Perils" section offers a brief overview of ecological and health concerns, even from a generally pro-biotech perspective.

10. Midwest Sustainable Agriculture Working Group, "MSAWG Position Paper on Genetic Engineering," 24 February 2000. Available at http//www.cfra.org/ MSAWG-GE.htm.

11. The London *Sunday Telegraph* on 10 October 1999 published "U.S. Alarm

Grows Over GM Foods, Congressmen Call for Labeling," in which they cite a Gallup poll reporting that 68 percent of adults surveyed want genetically engineered food labeled.

12. Miguel A. Altieri and Peter Rosset, *Ten Reasons Why Biotechnology Will Not Ensure Food Security, Protect the Environment and Reduce Poverty in the Developing World* (Oakland, Calif.: Food First/Institute for Food and Development Policy, October 1999).

13. The Rodale Institute, "Research at the Rodale Institute Challenges Toughest Critics of Organic." Press release, 15 March 2000.

14. One good organization that I'm familiar with is Vitamin Angel Alliance, at www.vitaminangel.com.

CHAPTER THIRTEEN

1. Norman Myers, "Subsidizing Environmental Damage," *Christian Science Monitor,* op-ed section, 17 April 2000. Myers suggests that U.S. taxpayers paid an average of more than $300 each in 1998 for government-paid subsidies to farmers that would otherwise have been included in the cost of food.

2. Organic Trade Association, "Questions and Answers About Organic," 13 March 2000. Available from OTA, www.ota.com, (413) 774-7511.

3. On average, Americans spend a smaller percentage of their annual income on food than most other citizens of the world. According to the American Farm Bureau, Americans spend about 10.9 percent of disposable income on food, compared to 11.2 percent in the United Kingdom, 14.5 percent in Sweden, 17.8 percent in Japan, 33.2 percent in Mexico, and 51.4 percent in India.

4. If you do agonize over paper versus plastic bags, *The Consumers Guide to Effective Environmental Choices,* by Michael Brower, Ph.D., and Warren Leon, Ph.D., of the Union of Concerned Scientists (New York: Three Rivers Press, 1999) says that the environmental costs are just about equal—you can make either choice work with recycling and reuse. They do, however, recommend that you try walking or taking public transportation to the store—and buy organic foods when possible.

5. See Resources for food safety links.

6. Consumers Union, "How Safe Is Our Produce?" *Consumer Reports* (March

1999). Available on-line at www.consumerreports.org/categories/foodhealth/ reports/9903peso.htm. "Peel those foods with high toxicity scores, such as apples, peaches, and pears. That usually removes much of the toxic residue. Washing with diluted dishwashing detergent also helps."

CHAPTER FOURTEEN

1. The law mandating this revised risk assessment is the Food Quality Protection Act (FQPA).

2. There are several references that support this. For a brief and accessible overview, see Consumers Union, "How Safe Is Our Produce?" *Consumer Reports* (March 1999), in the section entitled "Protecting Children."

3. For a more comprehensive and scientific look, see the various reports of Environmental Working Group (most with first author Richard Wiles) that pertain to children and pesticides, including "Overexposed" and "How 'Bout Them Apples?" (see Bibliography).

4. For a rigorous, scientific look at children's diets and chemicals, see John Wargo, *Our Children's Toxic Legacy* (New Haven, Conn.: Yale University Press, 1998), chapter 8, "The Susceptibility of Children," and chapter 9, "The Diet of a Child."

5. Ibid., 211. "Infants drink much more than they eat. Water intake is generally one order of magnitude greater than all other foods (other than breast milk during the first six months of life)."

6. The Environmental News Network reported on 9 August 1999 that Robert Hatherill, a researcher at the University of California, Santa Barbara, was calling for studies exploring the possible link between pesticides and youth violence.

7. Sandra Steingraber, *Living Downstream* (New York: Vintage Books, 1997, 1998), 39. "Cancer among children provides a particularly intimate glimpse into the possible routes of exposure to contaminants in the general environment and their possible significance for rising cancer rates among adults." Steingraber's book is a profound exploration of environmental toxins and health.

8. Theo Colborn et al., *Our Stolen Future* (New York: Dutton, 1996), 107.

9. Jane Houlihan and Richard Wiles, "Into the Mouths of Babes: Bottle-Fed Infants at Risk from Atrazine in Tap Water." (Washington, D.C.: Environmental Working Group/The Tides Center, 1999).

10. The Environmental Protection Agency upgraded atrazine to a "likely human carcinogen" in June 2000.

11. Marsha Walker, "Known Contaminants Found in Infant Formula," *Mothering* (May 2000): 67.

12. Theo Colborn et al., *Our Stolen Future* (New York: Dutton, 1996), 215–216. "It is premature to advise women against breast-feeding. . . . There is a pressing need for research to determine whether the concentrations of hormone-disrupting chemicals in human milk pose enough of a hazard to make breast-feeding inadvisable for some older women, perhaps those having their first child late in life. These older women will generally carry a much higher burden of persistent chemicals than first-time mothers who are twenty."

13. Consumers Union, "How Safe Is Our Produce?" *Consumer Reports* (March 1999). See also sidebars: "What Popeye Didn't Know" and "How They Scored."

14. Environmental Working Group, "A Shopper's Guide to Pesticides in Produce." On-line retrieval at www.ewg.org. EWG rates the twelve most contaminated foods (strawberries are number 1).

15. John Wargo, *Our Children's Toxic Legacy,* (New Haven, Conn.: Yale University Press, 1998), 173. "The most rapid periods of growth occur in utero, during infancy, and during puberty. . . . These periods of rapid growth may also be periods of heightened susceptibility."

16. Ibid., 205–206.

17. Richard Wiles and Kert Davies, "Pesticides in Baby Food" (Washington, D.C.: Environmental Working Group/The Tides Center, 1995), Executive Summary. Available at www.ewg.org/pub/home/reports/baby_food/baby_home.html.

18. Consumers Union, "How Safe Is Our Produce?" *Consumer Reports* (March 1999). Available at www.consumerreports.org/categories/foodhealth/reports/9903peso.htm.

19. Ibid.

20. Richard Wiles et al., "Overexposed: Organophosphate Insecticides in Children's Food" (Washington, D.C.: Environmental Working Group/The Tides Center, 1998): 1.

21. Beyond Pesticides/National Coalition Against the Misuse of Pesticides, "Environmentalists Urge Homeowners, Applicators and Farmers to Stop Use and Retailers to Stop Sale of Common Pesticide Subject to Partial Ban," Beyond Pesticides press release, 8 June 2000.

22. Sandra Steingraber, *Living Downstream* (New York: Vintage Books, 1997, 1998), 270–271.

23. Nation's Health, "Farm Children Face Exposure to Pesticides," *Nation's Health: The Official Newspaper of the American Public Health Association,* 1 June 2000.

24. Natural Resources Defense Council, "Trouble on the Farm: Growing Up with Pesticides in Agricultural Communities." New York: Natural Resources Defense Council, 1998.

25. Environmental Working Group, "About the Environmental Working Group." Available at www.ewg.org/about.html.

Bibliography

ALTIERI, MIGUEL A., and PETER ROSSET. *Ten Reasons Why Biotechnology Will Not Ensure Food Security, Protect the Environment and Reduce Poverty in the Developing World*. Oakland, Calif.: Food First/Institute for Food and Development Policy, October 1999. Available at http://www.foodfirst.org/resources/biotech/altieri-11-99.html. Retrieved 5 April 2000.

ANIMAL WELFARE INSTITUTE. "rBGH Ruled Unsafe for Canadian and European People and Cows." *Animal Welfare Institute Quarterly* 48, no. 2 (Spring 1999). Available at http://www. animalwelfare.com/farm/rbgh-s99.htm. Retrieved 18 March 2000.

BERRY, WENDELL. *Another Turn of the Crank*. Washington, D.C.: Counterpoint, 1995.

———. *What Are People For?* New York: North Point Press, 1990.

BOURNE, JOEL. "Bugging Out." *Audubon* (March/April 1999): 71–73.

———. "The Organic Revolution." *Audubon* (March/April 1999): 64–70.

BROWER, MICHAEL, and WARREN LEON. *The Consumer's Guide to Effective Environmental Choices: Practical Advice from the Union of Concerned Scientists*. New York: Three Rivers Press, 1999.

CARSON, RACHEL. *Silent Spring*. New York: Houghton Mifflin, 1962. With an introduction by Vice President Al Gore, 1994.

CENTER FOR INTEGRATED AGRICULTURAL SYSTEMS. "Research Brief #21: Community Supported Agriculture: Growing Food and Community." Center for Integrated Agricultural Systems, University of Wisconsin, Madison. Available at www. wisc.edu/cias/pubs/briefs/021.html. Revised 10 November 2000. Retrieved 27 November 2000.

CENTER FOR PUBLIC INTEGRITY. *Unreasonable Risk: The Politics of Pesticides*. Washington, D.C.: The Center for Public Integrity, 1998.

CLEEMANN, MARIANNE. "Persistent Organic Pollutants (POPs) in the Arctic Fauna." On-line site: Food Tables for Greenland. Available at www.dsf.gl/Inussuk/4foodtab/kap10.html. Retrieved 12 November 2000.

COLBORN, THEO, DIANNE DUMANOSKI, and JOHN PETERSON MYERS. *Our Stolen Future: Are We Threatening Our Fertility, Intelligence, and Survival?—A Scientific Detective Story*. New York: Dutton, 1996.

CONSUMERS UNION. "Greener Greens? The Truth About Organic Foods." *Consumer Reports* (January 1998): 12–18.

———. "How Safe Is Our Produce?" *Consumer Reports* (March 1999).

———. "Seeds of Change." *Consumer Reports* (September 1999): 41–46. Available at http://www.consumerreports.org. Retrieved 20 February 2000.

COOLEY, JACK P., and DANIEL A. LASS. "What's Your Share Worth? Some Comparisons of CSA Share Cost Versus Retail Produce Value." Available at http://klaatu.oit.umass.edu/resec/fac+staff/csa2.html. Retrieved 26 August 2000.

DIVER, STEVE. *Nutritional Quality of Organically Grown Food*. Fayetteville, Ark.: Appropriate Technology Transfer for Rural Areas, September 2000. Available at http://ncatark.uark.edu/~steved/food-quality.html. Retrieved 26 November 2000.

EARTH PLEDGE FOUNDATION, comp. *Sustainable Cuisine White Papers*. New York: Earth Pledge Foundation, 1999.

ENVIRONMENTAL WORKING GROUP. "A Shopper's Guide to Pesticides in Produce." Available at http://www.ewg.org

ERVIN, DAVID E., et al. "Agriculture and Environment: A New Strategic Vision." *Environment* 40, no. 6 (July/August 1998). Available at http://www.northernlight.com. Retrieved 4 December 1998. Northern Light Document No. LW19980812020014825.

FAGIN, DAN, MARIANNE LAVELLE, and the CENTER FOR PUBLIC INTEGRITY. *Toxic Deception: How the Chemical Industry Manipulates Science, Bends the Law and Endangers Your Health*. Monroe, Maine: Common Courage Press, 1999.

FELDMANN, MATTHEW, MICHAEL MORRIS, and DAVID HOISINGTON. "Why So Much Controversy Over Genetically Modified Organisms? Answers to 10 Frequently Asked Questions About GMOs." International Maize and Wheat Improvement Center (CIMMYT), 7 February 2000. Available at http://www.cimmyt.mx/research/abc/10-faqaboutgmos/htm/10-faqaboutgmos.htm. Retrieved 10 June 2000 and 26 November 2000.

FETTO, JOHN. "Home on the Organic Range." *American Demographics* (August 1999). Available at http://www.demographics.com/publications/AD/99_ad/9908_ad/ad990810.htm. Retrieved 29 January 2001.

FULWOOD, CHARLES. "Right from the Start: The Case Against Alar." Natural Resources Defense Council. Available at http://mail.igc.apc.org/nrdc/article/cfalar.html. Revised 5 February 1997. Retrieved 27 January 2000.

GIULIANO, JACKIE ALAN. "Toxic Bodies: Endocrine Disruption and Our Imperiled Future." *Environment News Service* (July 2000). Available at http://ens.lycos.com/ens/jul2000/2000L-07-31g.html. Retrieved 1 August 2000.

GORELICK, STEVEN. "Facing the Farm Crisis." *The Ecologist* 30, no. 4 (June 2000): 28–32.

———. "Solutions for a Farming Future." *The Ecologist* 30, no. 4 (June 2000): 34–35.

GREENE, CATHERINE. "U.S. Organic Agriculture Gaining Ground." *Agricultural Outlook* (April 2000): 9. A publication of the Economic Research Service of the USDA.

GUSSOW, JOAN DYE. "But Is It More Nutritious?" *Eating Well* (May/June 1997): 37–38.

HALPERN, DANIEL, ed. *Not for Bread Alone: Writers on Food, Wine, and the Art of Eating.* Hopewell, N.J.: Ecco Press, 1993.

HANSON, VICTOR DAVIS. *Fields Without Dreams: Defending the Agrarian Idea.* New York: Free Press, 1996.

———. *The Land Was Everything: Letters from an American Farmer.* New York: Free Press, 2000.

HART, MICHAEL. "I Feel Like a Cheat and a Failure." *The Ecologist* 30, no. 4 (June 2000): 33.

HARTMAN & NEW HOPE. *The Evolving Organic Marketplace.* Bellevue, Wash.: Hartman & New Hope, 1997.

HAWKEN, PAUL. *The Ecology of Commerce: A Declaration of Sustainability.* New York: HarperCollins, 1993.

HEARNE, SHELLEY A. *Harvest of Unknowns: Pesticide Contamination in Imported Foods.* New York: Natural Resources Defense Council, 1984.

HENDRIX, STEVE. "Chocolate Takes Flight." *International Wildlife* 28, no. 5 (October 1998). Available at http://www.northernlight.com. Retrieved 19 March 2000. Northern Light Document ID PN19980928010000230.

HETTENBACH, TODD, and RICHARD WILES. *Attack of the Killer Weeds: Pesticide Hyprocrisy on Capitol Hill.* Washington, D.C.: Environmental Working Group/The Tides Center, 1999.

———. *A Few Bad Apples . . . Pesticides in Your Produce: Why Supermarkets Should "Test and Tell."* Washington, D.C.: Environmental Working Group, 2000.

HEYMAN, HARRIET. "Harvest for the Rootless: Urban Gardens Pay Dividends to the Homeless." *Garden Design*, n.d.

HOULIHAN, JANE, and RICHARD WILES. *Into the Mouths of Babes: Bottle-Fed Infants at Risk from Atrazine in Tap Water.* Washington, D.C.: Environmental Working Group/The Tides Center, 1999.

JACKSON, WES. *Becoming Native to This Place.* Washington, D.C.: Counterpoint, 1994, 1996.

KINGSNORTH, PAUL. "Bovine Growth Hormones." *The Ecologist* 28, no. 5 (October 1998). Available at http://www.northernlight.com. Retrieved 18 March 2000. Northern Light Document ID PN19981118010000701.

KLINE, GARY. "Biodiversity and Development." *Journal of Third World Studies* 15, no. 1 (April 1998). Available at http://www.northernlight.com. Retrieved 26 November 2000. Northern Light Document No. BM19981026010067395.

KLONSKY, KAREN, and LAURA TOURTE. "Organic Agricultural Production in the United States: Debates and Directions (Emergence of U.S. Organic Agriculture)." *American Journal of Agricultural Economics* 80, no. 5 (December 1998). Available at http://northernlight.com. Retrieved 5 March 2000. Northern Light Document ID PN19990309010006740.

LEVY, BRIAN. "Seeding Power: The Other Problem with Genetically Modified Crops." *New Rules Journal* 2, no. 1 (Summer 2000). Available at http://www.newrules.org/generic_pages/nrsum00gmo.html. Retrieved 23 August 2000.

LIPSON, ELAINE. "A Brief History of the National Organic Standards." *California Certified Organic Farmers Newsletter* 15, no. 1 (Spring 1998): 4–11.

———. "A Delicious Inheritance." *Natural Foods Merchandiser* 21, no. 3 (March 2000): 95, 102–104.

———. "Community Supported Agriculture Links Consumers and Farmers." *Natural Foods Merchandiser* 20, no. 7 (July 1999).

———. "Deep Roots: The Legacy of Organic Farming." *Delicious!* 14, no. 9 (September 1998): 38–43, 70–72.

———. "Organic Rules Again." *Natural Business LOHAS Journal* 1, no. (May/June 2000): 52–54.

———. "Organics: Are They Really Better?" *Delicious!* 13, no. 9 (September 1997): 38–42.

LIPSON, MARK. *Searching for the "O-Word": Analyzing the USDA Current Research Information System for Pertinence to Organic Farming.* Santa Cruz, Calif.: Organic Farming Research Foundation, 1997.

——. "The First 'Ecolabel': Lessons from the Organic Experience." Paper submitted to the proceedings of "Eco Labeling for California Winegrapes," Sacramento, Calif., February 1998.

MASUMOTO, DAVID MAS. *Epitaph for a Peach: Four Seasons on My Family Farm.* San Francisco: HarperCollins, 1995.

MATHER, ROBIN. *A Garden of Unearthly Delights: Bioengineering and the Future of Food.* New York: Dutton, 1995.

MATTINA, MARY JANE INCORVIA, WILLIAM IANNUCCI-BERGER, and LAURE DYKAS. "Chlordane Uptake and Its Translocation in Food Crops." *Journal of Agricultural and Food Chemistry* 48, no. 5 (15 May 2000). Available at http://pubs.acs.org/hotartcl/jafcau/2000/jf990566a_rev.html. Retrieved 26 November 2000.

MEADOWS, DONELLA H. "A Load of Manure: The Arguments Against Organic Food—Why the Sudden Backlash?" On-line journal tompaine.common sense: Available at http://tompaine.com/opinion/2000/03/23/index.html. Retrieved 29 May 2000.

——. "Our Food, Our Future: Can Organic Farming Feed the World?" *Organic Gardening* (October 2000): 53–59.

MERGENTIME, KEN. "Organic Industry Roots Run Deep." *Organic Times/Natural Foods Merchandiser* (1994). Available at http://www.nfm-online.com/OT/OT_94?/OT_history.html. Retrieved 13 April 1999.

MIDWEST SUSTAINABLE AGRICULTURE WORKING GROUP. "Midwest Sustainable Agriculture Working Group Position Paper on Genetic Engineering" (24 February 2000). Available at http://www.cfra.org/MSAWG-GE.htm. Retrieved 3 March 2000.

MITCHELL, JENNIFER. "Nowhere to Hide: The Global Spread of High-Risk Synthetic Chemicals." *World Watch* 10, no. 2 (March/April 1997). Available at http://www.northernlight.com. Retrieved 12 November 2000. Northern Light Document No. PC19970927160003778.

MYERS, NORMAN. "Subsidizing Environmental Damage." *Christian Science Monitor,* op-ed, 17 April 2000. Available at http://www.northernlight.com. Retrieved 12 November 2000. Northern Light Document ID UU2000410 7110086915.

MYERS, STEVE. "The Farmer in the Dell: A Review of Sustainable and Organic Farming Progress." *Organic and Natural News* 3, no. 8 (August 2000): 24–25.

NASH, J. MADELEINE. "Grains of Hope." *Time* 156, no. 5 (31 July 2000): 38–46.

NATURAL RESOURCES DEFENSE COUNCIL. "America's Animal Factories: How States Fail to Prevent Pollution from Livestock Waste," 1998. Available at http://www. nrdc.org/nrdc/nrdcpro/factor/exec.html. Retrieved 18 March 2000.

———. "Coffee, Conservation, and Commerce in the Western Hemisphere: How Individuals and Institutions Can Promote Ecologically Sound Farming and Forest Management in Northern Latin America." New York: Natural Resources Defense Council and Smithsonian Migratory Bird Center, 1996. Available at http://www. nrdc.org/nrdcpro/ccc/forew.html. Retrieved 19 March 2000.

———. "Eating What Comes Naturally." Available at http://www.nrdc.org/ health/farming/forg101.asp. Revised 15 April 2000. Retrieved 25 October 2000.

———. "Trouble on the Farm: Growing Up with Pesticides in Agricultural Communities," 1998. Available at http://www.nrdc.org/nrdc/nrdcpro/farm/ intro.html. Retrieved 18 March 2000.

ORGANIC TRADE ASSOCIATION. "Environmental Facts." "Business Facts." "Water Safety Facts." "Manure Use and Agricultural Practices." "Fact Sheet on *E. coli.*" "Questions and Answers About Organic." Available at http://www. ota.com. Retrieved 24 October 2000.

OWENS, KAGAN, and JAY FELDMAN. "The Schooling of State Pesticide Laws: Review of State Pesticide Laws Regarding Schools." *Pesticides and You* 18, no. 3 (1998): 9–22. Quarterly newsletter of Beyond Pesticides/National Coalition Against the Misuse of Pesticides.

PERRY, MELISSA J., and FREDERICK R. BLOOM. "Perceptions of Pesticide-Associated Cancer Risks Among Farmers: A Qualitative Assessment." *Human Organization* 57, no. 3 (1998). Available at http://www.northernlight.com. Retrieved 6 February 2000. Northern Light Document ID BM199810230 50000157.

POLLAN, MICHAEL. "Playing God in the Garden." *New York Times Magazine,* 25 October 1998.

REPETTO, ROBERT, and SANJAY S. BALIGA. *Pesticides and the Immune System: The Public Health Risks.* Washington, D.C.: World Resources Institute, 1996.

RISSLER, JANE, and MARGARET MELLON. *The Ecological Risks of Engineered Crops.* Cambridge, Mass.: MIT Press, 1996.

RODALE INSTITUTE. "Research at the Rodale Institute Challenges Toughest Critics of Organic: Scientific Trials Prove Organic Agriculture Is Economically Competitive, Environmentally Friendly and Efficient." The Rodale Institute press release, 15 March 2000.

RODALE, MARIA, and ELLEN PHILLIPS. "Greener and Cleaner." *Audubon* 101, no. 2 (March/April 1999): 80–83.

ROSSET, PETER, and VANDANA SHIVA. "Small-Scale Farming: A Global Perspective." *The Ecologist* 30, no. 4 (June 2000): 36–37.

SAMPAT, PAYAL. "Groundwater Shock: The Polluting of the World's Major Freshwater Stores." *World Watch* 13, no. 1 (January/February 2000): 10–22.

SANDERS, SCOTT RUSSELL. "Lessons from the Land Institute." *Audubon* 101, no. 2 (March/April 1999): 74–79.

SCHETTLER, TED, et al., eds. *Generations at Risk: Reproductive Health and the Environment.* Cambridge, Mass.: MIT Press, 1999.

SCULLY, MALCOLM G. "The Destructive Nature of Our Bountiful Harvests." *The Chronicle of Higher Education* 46, no. 24 (18 February 2000): B11–B12. Available at http://www.landinstitute.org/harvests.html. Retrieved through www.landinstitute.org, 12 November 2000.

SHAPIRO, HOWARD-YANA, and JOHN HARRISON. *Gardening for the Future of the Earth.* New York: Bantam Books, 2000.

SHISTAR, TERRY, SUSAN COOPER, and JAY FELDMAN. *Unnecessary Risks: The Benefit Side of the Pesticide Risk-Benefit Equation.* Washington, D.C.: National Coalition Against the Misuse of Pesticides, 1992.

SMITHSONIAN MIGRATORY BIRD CENTER. "Why Migratory Birds Are Crazy for Coffee." Available at http://natzoo.si.edu/smbc/fxshts/fxsht1a.htm. Retrieved 26 November 2000.

SOIL ASSOCIATION. "Briefing Paper: Organic Facts and Figures, May 2000." Available at http://www.soilassociation.org. Retrieved 12 November 2000.

———. "Briefing Sheet: The Biodiversity Benefits of Organic Farming: Executive Summary and Report." Available at http://www.soilassociation.org. Retrieved 12 November 2000.

SOULE, JUDY, DANIELLE CARRE, and WES JACKSON. "Ecological Impact of Modern Agriculture." New York: McGraw-Hill, 1990, 165–188. Available at http://www.eap.mcgill.ca/DIAE_1.htm. Retrieved 4 December 1998.

STEINGRABER, SANDRA. *Living Downstream: A Scientist's Personal Investigation of Cancer and the Environment*. New York: Vintage Books, 1998.

THOMPSON, GARY D. "Consumer Demand for Organic Foods: What We Know and What We Need to Know." *American Journal of Agricultural Economics* 80, no. 5 (1998): 1113–1118.

UNITED STATES DEPARTMENT OF AGRICULTURE AGRICULTURAL MARKETING SERVICE. "AMS Farmers Markets Facts." Available at http://www.ams.usda.gov/farmersmarkets/facts.htm. Revised 16 February 2000. Retrieved 3 October 2000.

———. "7 CFR Part 205: National Organic Program; Proposed Rule." *Federal Register* 65, no. 49 (13 March 2000): 13513–13658.

UNITED STATES DEPARTMENT OF AGRICULTURE NATIONAL ORGANIC PROGRAM. "Final Rule." 2000. Available at http://www.ams.usda.gov/nop/nop2000/nopfinalrulepages/finalrulemap.htm. Also published in *Federal Register* 65, no. 246 (21 December 2000).

WALKER, MARSHA. "Known Contaminants Found in Infant Formula." *Mothering* (May 2000): 67. Available at http://www.northernlight.com. Retrieved 2 September 2000. Northern Light Document ID UU20000523150012706.

WALZ, ERICA. *Final Results of the Third Biennial National Organic Farmers' Survey*. Santa Cruz, Calif.: Organic Farming Research Foundation, 1999.

WARGO, JOHN. *Our Children's Toxic Legacy: How Science and Law Fail to Protect Us from Pesticides*. 2d ed. New Haven, Conn.: Yale University Press, 1998.

WATERS, CHRISTINA. "Preserving the Past: Heirloom Vegetables Offer Us a Magnificent Array of Old-World Flavors." *Vegetarian Times*, no. 252 (August 1998). Available at http://www.northernlight.com. Retrieved 26 December 1999. Northern Light Document ID LW19980916140002775.

WILES, RICHARD, ET AL. "Same as It Ever Was . . . The Clinton Administration's 1993 Pesticide Reduction Policy in Perspective." Washington, D.C.: Environmental Working Group/The Tides Center, 1998.

———. "How 'Bout Them Apples? Pesticides in Children's Food Ten Years After Alar." Washington, D.C.: Environmental Working Group/The Tides Center, 1999.

WILES, RICHARD, and KERT DAVIES. "Pesticides in Baby Food." Washington, D.C.: Environmental Working Group/The Tides Foundation, 1995. Available at http://www.ewg.org/pub/home/reports/baby_food/baby_home.html. Retrieved 3 September 2000.

WILES, RICHARD, KERT DAVIES, and CHRISTOPHER CAMPBELL. "Overexposed: Organophosphate Insecticides in Children's Food." Washington, D.C.: Environmental Working Group/The Tides Center, 1998.

WILES, RICHARD, KERT DAVIES, and SUSAN ELDERKIN. "A Shopper's Guide to Pesticides in Produce." Washington, D.C.: Environmental Working Group. Available at http://www.ewg.org/pub/home/reports/Shoppers/Shoppers.html. Retrieved 22 August 2000.

Index